Magento PHP Developer's Guide

Get started with the flexible and powerful e-commerce framework, Magento

Allan MacGregor

PUBLISHING

BIRMINGHAM - MUMBAI

Magento PHP Developer's Guide

First published: April 2013

Production Reference: 1250313

Published by Packt Publishing Ltd.
Livery Place
35 Livery Street
Birmingham B3 2PB, UK.

ISBN 978-1-78216-306-0

www.packtpub.com

Cover Image by Sandeep Babu (sandyjb@gmail.com)

Credits

Author
Allan MacGregor

Reviewers
Jay El-Kaake

Michael K. Kreitzer

Corey Slavnik

Acquisition Editor
Edward Gordon

Lead Technical Editor
Azharuddin Sheikh

Technical Editors
Devdutt Kulkarni

Kaustubh S. Mayekar

Ankita R. Meshram

Project Coordinator
Anugya Khurana

Proofreader
Jonathan Todd

Indexer
Tejal Soni

Graphics
Aditi Gajjar

Production Coordinator
Arvindkumar Gupta

Cover Work
Arvindkumar Gupta

About the Author

Allan MacGregor is a Magento Certified Developer Plus with four years of Magento experience. He also has a certification in Linux System Administration by IBM.

He started working with Magento as a freelance looking for a better framework to build e-commerce solutions, and he is now the Magento Lead Developer at Demac Media (`www.demacmedia.com`). He's very passionate about software development in general. He is constantly working with new technologies and frameworks.

At Demac Media, he has participated in building core solutions for a wide range of clients; this has given him the experience and knowledge to solve many Magento challenges.

As part of an internal project at Demac Media, he worked on Triplecheck.io (`www.triplecheck.io`), a unique service for monitoring and auditing the code health of a Magento store. You can also follow him on Twitter at `http://www.twitter.com/allanmacgregor`.

Writing this book has been a demanding experience but full of rewards. While writing, I have discovered more of Magento and a little bit more of myself, both as a person and a developer.

First and foremost, I want to thank my amazing wife for her unconditional support and understanding while working on these projects.

To Matthew Bertulli and Dimitri Colomvakos, co-founders of Demac Media, for all their support.

To my co-workers and friends, Michael Krietzer and Corey Slavnik, who kindly volunteered their time and effort to review this book.

And special thanks to the whole Demac Media family.

This wouldn't be possible without any of you.

About the Reviewers

Jay El-Kaake started his first tech entrepreneurship adventure at the age of 10 when he developed and launched his first website. Now, as a Co-founder and CEO of Sweet Tooth Inc, Jay oversees up to 1,000 Magento stores per year as Sweet Tooth's client base of over 3,000 Magento e-commerce clients grows.

Through his role at Sweet Tooth Inc., Jay was the lead in developing some of the most popular extensions of Magento: Sweet Tooth Rewards, a full-featured loyalty and rewards program extension; Better Store Search, a turn-key product search optimizer; Better Store CMS, a Magento CMS improver; and Enhanced Grid, the second most downloaded community-written extension for Magento with over 70,000 installations.

Jay's GitHub account can be found at `https://github.com/jayelkaake`.

You can also follow Jay on Twitter at `http://www.twitter.com/jayelkaake`.

Michael K. Kreitzer, born in Chatham, Ontario, and raised in the small town of Thamesville, began his journey in the IT industry at an early age from the moment he wrote his first *Hello World* program. He studied Computer Programming at Sheridan College in Oakville, Ontario and is now a Magento Certified Plus Developer at Demac Media Inc. He lives in Mississauga, Ontario with his wife Megan and dog Padme.

> I would like to thank my family for their love and support, as well as my co-workers who help me continue to learn every day.

Corey Slavnik is a Certified Magento Developer from Toronto, Ontario. He understood his affinity for programming at a young age when he built games in RPG Maker 2000. He attended McMaster University for his undergraduate degree and continued to learn (and love) Magento at Demac Media. Corey also enjoys craft beer and yoga.

I would like to thank my parents for always pushing me to pursue great opportunities, and my co-workers, who have helped me learn all things about Magento.

www.PacktPub.com

Support files, eBooks, discount offers and more

You might want to visit www.PacktPub.com for support files and downloads related to your book.

Did you know that Packt offers eBook versions of every book published, with PDF and ePub files available? You can upgrade to the eBook version at www.PacktPub.com and as a print book customer, you are entitled to a discount on the eBook copy. Get in touch with us at service@packtpub.com for more details.

At www.PacktPub.com, you can also read a collection of free technical articles, sign up for a range of free newsletters and receive exclusive discounts and offers on Packt books and eBooks.

http://PacktLib.PacktPub.com

Do you need instant solutions to your IT questions? PacktLib is Packt's online digital book library. Here, you can access, read and search across Packt's entire library of books.

Why Subscribe?

- Fully searchable across every book published by Packt
- Copy and paste, print and bookmark content
- On demand and accessible via web browser

Free Access for Packt account holders

If you have an account with Packt at www.PacktPub.com, you can use this to access PacktLib today and view nine entirely free books. Simply use your login credentials for immediate access.

Table of Contents

Preface

The *Magento PHP Developer's Guide* will help new and not so new developers to understand and work with Magento's fundamental concepts and standard practices for developing and testing code in Magento.

This book is my attempt to write a guide that answers questions that many developers, including myself, had when we started to develop for Magento: What is EAV? How does the ORM in Magento work? What are observers and events? Which design patterns were used to create Magento?

Most importantly, this book also answers questions that many developer still have to this day: What is the standard for developing modules and extending the frontend and backend? How can I properly test my code? What is the best method to deploy and distribute custom modules?

What this book covers

Chapter 1, Understanding and Setting Up Our Development Environment, will help you set up a complete environment for Magento development with MySQL and Apache. Additionally, we will go over the tools available to facilitate the development, several IDEs, and version control systems.

Chapter 2, Magento Fundamentals for Developers, will be about the fundamental concepts of Magento, such as the system architecture, MVC implementation, and its relation with Zend Framework. All the concepts in this chapter will set the foundation for developers starting with Magento.

Chapter 3, ORM and Data Collections, covers collections and models in Magento that are the bread and butter of everyday Magento development. In this chapter, we will introduce the reader to the Magento ORM system, and we will learn how to properly work with data collections and the EAV system.

Chapter 4, Frontend Development, will explain the practical use of the skills and knowledge we have acquired so far, and we'll be building a fully functional Magento Module step by step. The custom module will allow readers to apply a variety of important concepts, such as working with collections, routing, sessions, and caching.

Chapter 5, Backend Development, will extend what we built in the previous chapter and create an interface in the Magento backend for interacting with our application data. We will learn about extending the backend, the admin HTML theme, setting data sources, and controlling our extension behavior through configuration.

Chapter 6, The Magento API, will explain the Magento API and how we can extend it for providing access to the custom data that we captured using our extension.

Chapter 7, Testing and Quality Assurance, will help the reader learn critical skills for testing our Magento modules and custom, which form an integral part of development. We will learn about the different types of tests and the tools available for each particular type of test.

Chapter 8, Deployment and Distribution, will help the reader learn about the multiple tools available for deploying our code to a production environment and how to properly pack our extensions for distribution through channels such as Magento Connect.

Appendix, Hello Magento, will give new developers a quick and easy to follow introduction for creating our first Magento Extension.

What you need for this book

You will need an installation of Magento 1.7, either on a local machine or on a remote server, your favorite code editor, and permissions to install and modify files.

Who this book is for

If you are a PHP developer getting started with Magento or if you already have some experience with Magento and want to understand the Magento architecture and how to extend the frontend and backend of Magento, this is the book for you!

You are expected to be confident with PHP5. No experience with Magento Development is expected, although you should be familiar with basic Magento operations and concepts.

Conventions

In this book, you will find a number of styles of text that distinguish between different kinds of information. Here are some examples of these styles and an explanation of their meaning.

Code words in text are shown as follows: "GitHub now includes a `.gitignore` file specifically for Magento, which will ignore all the files in the Magento core and only keep track of our own code."

A block of code is set as follows:

```
{
    "id": "default",
    "host": "magento.localhost.com",
    "repo": [
        "url": "svn.magentocommerce.com/source/branches/1.7",
```

Any command-line input or output is written as follows:

```
$ vagrant box add lucid32 http://files.vagrantup.com/lucid32.box
$ vagrant init lucid32
$ vagrant up
```

New terms and **important words** are shown in bold. Words that you see on the screen, in menus or dialog boxes for example, appear in the text like this: "You should now see Apache's default web page with the message **It Works!**".

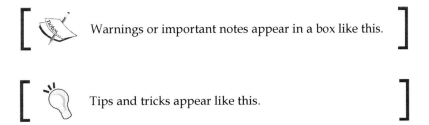

Warnings or important notes appear in a box like this.

Tips and tricks appear like this.

Reader feedback

Feedback from our readers is always welcome. Let us know what you think about this book—what you liked or may have disliked. Reader feedback is important for us to develop titles that you really get the most out of.

To send us general feedback, simply send an e-mail to feedback@packtpub.com, and mention the book title via the subject of your message.

If there is a topic that you have expertise in and you are interested in either writing or contributing to a book, see our author guide on www.packtpub.com/authors.

Customer support

Now that you are the proud owner of a Packt book, we have a number of things to help you to get the most from your purchase.

Downloading the example code

You can download the example code files for all Packt books you have purchased from your account at http://www.packtpub.com. If you purchased this book elsewhere, you can visit http://www.packtpub.com/support and register to have the files e-mailed directly to you.

Errata

Although we have taken every care to ensure the accuracy of our content, mistakes do happen. If you find a mistake in one of our books—maybe a mistake in the text or the code—we would be grateful if you would report this to us. By doing so, you can save other readers from frustration and help us improve subsequent versions of this book. If you find any errata, please report them by visiting http://www.packtpub.com/submit-errata, selecting your book, clicking on the **errata submission form** link, and entering the details of your errata. Once your errata are verified, your submission will be accepted and the errata will be uploaded on our website, or added to any list of existing errata, under the Errata section of that title. Any existing errata can be viewed by selecting your title from http://www.packtpub.com/support.

Piracy

Piracy of copyright material on the Internet is an ongoing problem across all media. At Packt, we take the protection of our copyright and licenses very seriously. If you come across any illegal copies of our works, in any form, on the Internet, please provide us with the location address or website name immediately so that we can pursue a remedy.

Please contact us at copyright@packtpub.com with a link to the suspected pirated material.

We appreciate your help in protecting our authors, and our ability to bring you valuable content.

Questions

You can contact us at questions@packtpub.com if you are having a problem with any aspect of the book, and we will do our best to address it.

1
Understanding and Setting Up Our Development Environment

In this chapter, we will go over the stack of technologies involved in running Magento and how to set up a proper environment for development. The following topics will be covered in this chapter:

- LAMP virtual machine
- Setting up and using VirtualBox
- Setting up and using Vagrant
- IDEs and version control systems

We will also learn how to set up a LAMP virtual machine from scratch and how to automate this process entirely using Vagrant and Chef.

LAMP from scratch

LAMP (Linux, Apache, MySQL, and PHP) is a solution stack of open source technologies, which is used for building a web server and is also the current standard for running Magento.

For a more detailed list of requirements, please visit `www.magentocommerce.com/ system-requirements`.

 Although Nginx has seen a wider range of adoption among Magento developers at the time of writing this book, Apache2 is still the community-accepted standard. We will focus on working with it.

As developers, there are multiple challenges and nuances of setting and maintaining our development environment, such as:

- Matching your development and production environments
- Keeping a consistent environment between different platforms and team members
- Setting up a new environment that takes several hours
- Not all developers have the knowledge or experience for setting up a LAMP server on their own

We can resolve the first two points with the help of Oracle's VirtualBox (www.virtualbox.org). VirtualBox is a powerful and widely popular virtualization engine that will allow us to create **virtual machines** (**VMs**). VMs can also be shared between developers and across all major operating systems.

Getting VirtualBox

VirtualBox is open source, and it is supported across all platforms. It can be downloaded directly from www.virtualbox.org/wiki/Downloads.

Now, we will proceed to setting up a Linux virtual machine. We have selected Ubuntu Server 12.04.2 LTS for its ease of use and widely available support. First, download the ISO file from www.ubuntu.com/download/server; both 64-bit and 32-bit versions will work.

To create a new Linux virtual machine, perform the following steps:

1. Start **VirtualBox Manager** and click on the **New** button in the upper-left corner, as shown in the following screenshot:

2. A wizard dialog will pop up and will guide us through the steps for creating a bare virtual machine. The wizard will ask us for the basic information for setting up the virtual machine:

    ° **VM Name**: How shall we name our virtual machine? Let's name it Magento_dev 01.

    ° **Memory**: This is the value of system memory that will be assigned to the guest operating system when our VM starts; for running a full LAMP server, 1 GB or more is recommended.

- ○ **Operating System Type**: This is the type of OS that we will be installing later; in our case, we want to select **Linux/Ubuntu**, and depending on our selection, VirtualBox will enable or disable certain VM options.

3. Next, we need to specify a virtual hard disk. Select **Create a virtual hard drive now**, as shown in the following screenshot:

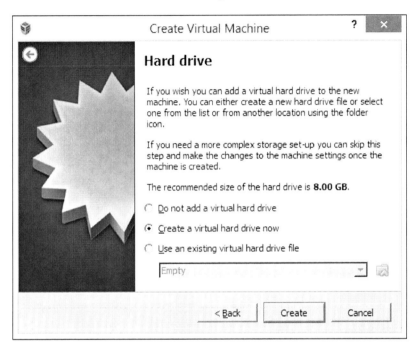

4. There are many hard disk options available, but for most purposes, selecting **VirtualBox Disk Image** (**VDI**) will suffice. This will create a single file on our host operating system.

5. We now need to select the type of storage on the physical drive. We are provided with the following two options:

- ○ **Dynamically Allocated**: The disk image will grow automatically as the number of files and usage on our guest operating system grows

- ○ **Fixed Size**: This option will limit the size of the virtual disk from the start

6. Next, we will need to specify the size of our virtual hard disk. We want to adjust the size depending on how many Magento installations we plan to use.

In general, we want to keep at least 2 GB per Magento installation, and another 3 GB if we are running the database server on the same installation. This is not to say that all that space will be used at once or even at all, but Magento installations can use a lot of disk space once product images and cache files are factored in.

7. Finally, we just need to click on the **Create** button.

 The main difference is that the fixed-size hard disk will reserve the space on the physical hard drive right from the start, whereas the dynamically allocated hard disk will grow incrementally until it acquires the specified size.

The newly created box will appear on the left-hand side navigation menu, but before starting our recently created VM, we need to make some changes, as follows:

i. Select our newly created VM and click on the **Settings** button at the top.

ii. Open the **Network** menu and select **Adapter 2**. We will set **Attached to** to **Bridged Adapter** as we want to set this up as a bridged adapter to our main network interface. This will allow us to connect remotely using SSH.

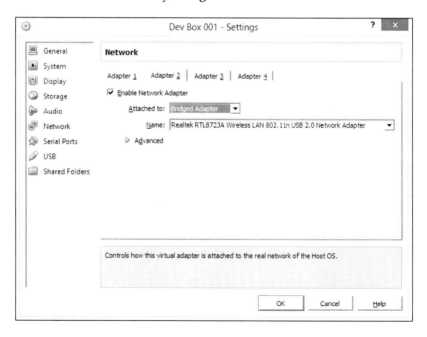

iii. Go to the **System** menu and change the boot order so that the CD/DVD-ROM boots first.

iv. On the **Storage** menu, select one of the empty IDE controllers and mount our previously downloaded Ubuntu ISO image.

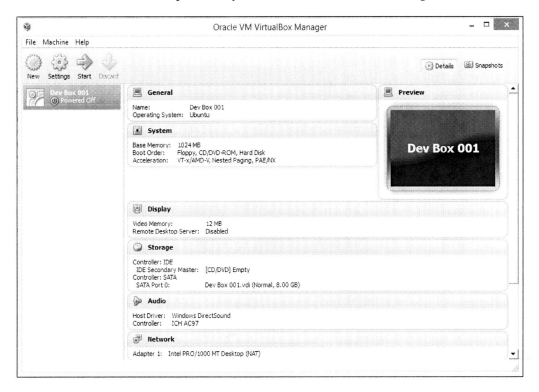

Booting our virtual machine

At this point, we have successfully installed and configured our VirtualBox instance, and we are now ready to boot our new virtual machine for the first time. To do this, just select the VM in the left sidebar and click on the **Start** button at the top.

A new window will pop up with an interface to the VM. Ubuntu will take a few minutes to boot up.

Once Ubuntu has finished booting up, we will see two menus. The first menu will allow us to select the language, and the second one is the main menu, which provides several options. In our case, we just want to proceed with the **Install Ubuntu Server** option.

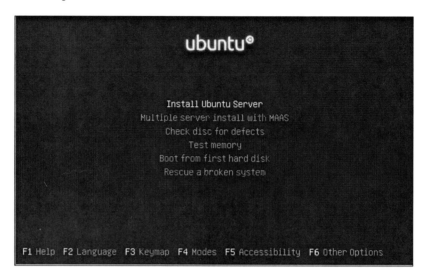

We should now see the Ubuntu installation wizard, which will ask for our language and keyboard settings; after selecting the appropriate settings for our country and language, the installer will proceed to load all the necessary packages in memory. This can take up a few minutes.

Ubuntu will proceed to configure our main network adapter, and once the automatic configuration is done, we will be asked to set up the hostname for the virtual machine. We can leave the hostname to default settings.

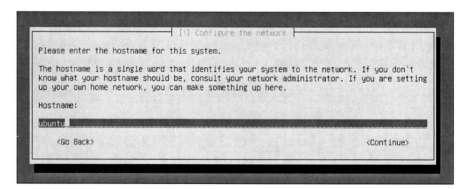

The next screen will request us to enter the full name of our user; for this example, let's use `Magento Developer`:

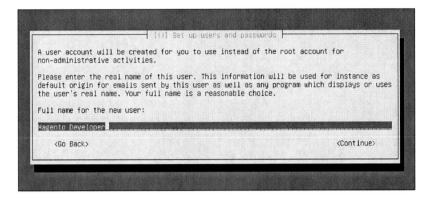

Next, we will be asked to create a username and password. Let's use `magedev` as our username:

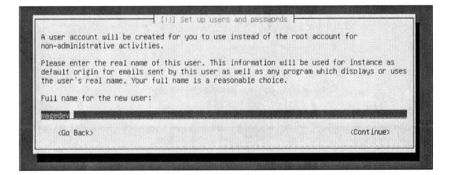

And let's use `magento2013` as our password:

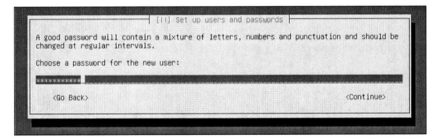

On the next screens, we will be asked to confirm our password and set up the correct time zone; after entering the right values, the installation wizard will show the following screen asking about our partition settings:

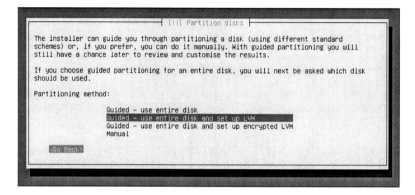

In our case, we select **Guided – use entire disk and set up LVM**; let's now confirm that we are partitioning our virtual disk:

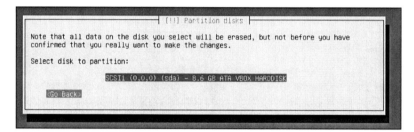

We will be asked to confirm our changes a final time; select **Finish partitioning and write changes to disk,** as shown in the following screenshot:

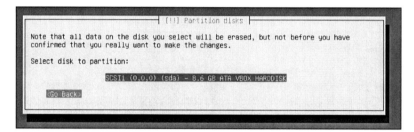

The installation wizard will ask us to select predefined packages to install; one of the options available is **LAMP server**.

Although this is highly convenient, we don't want to install the LAMP server that comes pre-packaged with our Ubuntu CD; we will be installing all the LAMP components manually to guarantee that they are set up according to specific needs and are up to date with the latest patches.

Next, for this, we will need an SSH server; select **OpenSSH server** from the list and click on **Continue**:

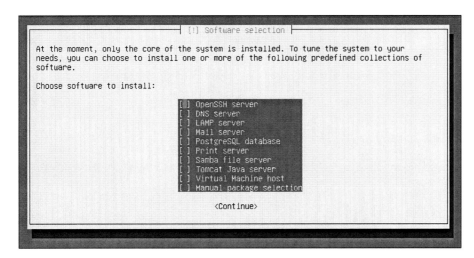

Now, installation of Ubuntu is complete and it will reboot into our newly installed virtual box.

We are almost ready to proceed with the installation of the rest of our environment, but first we need to update our package manager repository definitions, log in to the console and run the following command:

```
$ sudo apt-get update
```

APT stands for **Advanced Packaging Tool** and is one of the core libraries included with most Debian GNU/Linux distributions; apt greatly simplifies the process of installing and maintaining software on our systems.

Once apt-get has finished updating all the repository sources, we can proceed with the installation of the other components of our LAMP server.

Installing Apache2

Apache is an HTTP server. Currently, it is used to host over 60 percent of the websites on the Web and is the accepted standard for running Magento stores. There are many guides and tutorials available online for fine-tuning and tweaking Apache2 for increasing Magento performance.

Installing Apache is as simple as running the following command:

```
$ sudo apt-get install apache2 -y
```

This will take care of installing Apache2 and all the required dependencies for us. If everything has been installed correctly, we can now test by opening our browser and entering http://192.168.36.1/.

Apache by default runs as a service and can be controlled with the following commands:

```
$ sudo apache2ctl stop
$ sudo apache2ctl start
$ sudo apache2ctl restart
```

You should now see Apache's default web page with the message **It Works!**.

Installing PHP

PHP is a server-side scripting language and stands for **PHP Hypertext Processor**. Magento is implemented on PHP5 and Zend Framework, and we would need to install PHP and some additional libraries in order to run it.

Let's use apt-get again and run the following commands to get php5 and all the necessary libraries installed:

```
$ sudo apt-get install php5 php5-curl php5-gd php5-imagick php5-imap
php5-mcrypt php5-mysql -y
$ sudo apt-get install php-pear php5-memcache -y
$ sudo apt-get install libapache2-mod-php5 -y
```

The first command installed, not only php5, but also additional packages required by Magento to connect with our database and manipulate images.

The second command will install PEAR, a PHP package manager and a PHP memcached adapter.

 Memcached is a high-performance, distributed memory caching system; this is an optional caching system for Magento.

The third command installs and sets up the php5 module for Apache.

We can finally test that our PHP installation is working by running the following command:

```
$ php -v
```

Installing MySQL

MySQL is a popular choice of database for many web applications, and Magento is no exception. We will need to install and set up MySQL as part of development stack using the following command:

```
$ sudo apt-get install mysql-server mysql-client -y
```

During installation, we will be asked to enter a root password; use magento2013. Once the installer has finished, we should have a mysql service instance running in the background. We can test it by trying to connect to the mysql server using the following command:

```
$ sudo mysql -uroot -pmagento2013
```

If everything has been installed correctly, we should see the following mysql server prompt:

```
mysql>
```

At this point, we have a fully functional LAMP environment that can be used not only for developing and working on Magento websites but also for any other kind of PHP development.

Putting everything together

At this point, we have a basic LAMP set up and running. However, for working with Magento, we would need to do some configuration changes and additional setup.

The first thing that we will need to do is to create a location to store our development site's files, so we will run the following commands:

```
$ sudo mkdir -p /srv/www/magento_dev/public_html/
$ sudo mkdir /srv/www/magento_dev/logs/
$ sudo mkdir /srv/www/magento_dev/ssl/
```

This will create the necessary folder structure for our first Magento site. Now we need to check out the latest version of Magento. We can quickly get the files by using SVN.

We would first need to install SVN on our server with the following command:

```
$ sudo apt-get install subversion -y
```

Once the installer has finished, open the magento_dev directory and run the svn command to get the latest version files:

```
$ cd /srv/www/magento_dev
$ sudo svn export --force http://svn.magentocommerce.com/source/
branches/1.7 public_html/
```

We will also need to fix some of the permissions on our new Magento copy:

```
$ sudo chown -R www-data:www-data public_html/
$ sudo chmod -R 755 public_html/var/
$ sudo chmod -R 755 public_html/media/
$ sudo chmod -R 755 public_html/app/etc/
```

Next, we need to create a new database for our Magento installation. Let's open our mysql shell:

```
$ sudo mysql -uroot -pmagento2013
```

Once in the mysql shell, we can use the create command, which should be followed by the type of entity (database, table) we want to create and the database name to create a new database:

```
mysql> create database magento_dev;
```

Although we could use the root credentials for accessing our development database, this is not a recommended practice to follow because it could compromise not only a single site but also the full database server. MySQL accounts are restricted based on privileges. We want to create a new set of credentials that has limited privileges to only our working database:

```
mysql> GRANT ALL PRIVILEGES ON magento_dev.* TO 'mage'@'localhost'
IDENTIFIED BY 'dev2013$#';
```

Now, we need to properly set up Apache2 and enable some additional modules; fortunately, this version of Apache comes with a set of useful commands:

- a2ensite: This creates symlinks between the vhost files in the sites-available and the sites-enabled folders to allow the Apache Server to read those files.
- a2dissite: This removes the symlinks created by the a2ensite command. This effectively disables the site.
- a2enmod: This is used to create symlinks between the mods-enabled directory and the module configuration files.
- a2dismod: This will remove the symlinks from mods-enabled directory. This command will prevent the module from being loaded by Apache.

Magento uses the mod_rewrite module for generating the URLs. mod_rewrite uses a rule-based rewriting engine to rewrite request URLs on the fly.

We can enable mod_rewrite with the a2enmod command:

```
$ sudo a2enmod rewrite
```

The next step will require that we create a new virtual host file under the sites-available directory:

```
$ sudo nano /etc/apache2/sites-available/magento.localhost.com
```

The nano command will open a shell text editor where we can set up the configuration for our virtual domain:

```
<VirtualHost *:80>
  ServerAdmin magento@locahost.com
  ServerName magento.localhost.com
  DocumentRoot /srv/www/magento_dev/public_html

  <Directory /srv/www/magento_dev/public_html/>
    Options Indexes FollowSymlinks MultiViews
    AllowOverride All
    Order allow,deny
```

```
      allow from all
   </Directory>
   ErrorLog /srv/www/magento_dev/logs/error.log
   LogLevel warn
</VirtualHost>
```

To save the new virtual host file, press *Ctrl + O* and then *Ctrl + X*. The virtual host file will tell Apache where it can find the site files and what permissions to give them. In order for the new configuration changes to take effect, we need to enable the new site and restart Apache. We can use the following commands to do so:

```
$ sudo a2ensite magento.localhost.com
```

```
$ sudo apache2ctl restart
```

We are nearly ready to install Magento. We just need to set up a local mapping into our host system host file by using any of the following:

- Windows
    i.   Open `C:\system32\drivers\etc\hosts` in notepad
    ii. Add the following line at the end of the file:
         `192.168.36.1 magento.localhost.com`

- Unix/Linux/OSX
    i.   Open `/etc/hosts` using `nano`:
         ```
         $ sudo nano /etc/hosts
         ```
    ii. Add the following line at the end of the file:
         `192.168.36.1 magento.localhost.com`

 If you are having problems making the necessary changes to your host files, please Visit `http://www.magedevguide.com/hostfile-help`.

We can now install Magento by opening `http://magento.localhost.com` in our browser. At last, we should see the installation wizard. Follow the steps as indicated by the wizard, and you will be set to go!

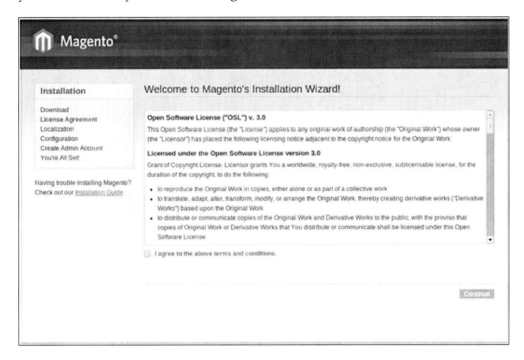

Up and running with Vagrant

Previously, we created a Magento install using a VM. Although using a VM gives us a reliable environment, setting our LAMP for each of our Magento staging installations can still be very complicated. This is especially true for developers without experience working on a Unix/Linux environment.

What if we could get all the benefits of running a VM, but with a completely automated setup process? What if we were able to have new VM instances created and configured on the fly for each of our staging websites?

This is possible by using Vagrant in combination with Chef. We can create automated VMs without the need of having an extensive knowledge about Linux or the different LAMP components.

 Vagrant currently supports VirtualBox 4.0.x, 4.1.x, and 4.2.x.

Installing Vagrant

Vagrant can be downloaded directly from `downloads.vagrantup.com`. Furthermore, its packages and installers are available for multiple platforms. Once you download Vagrant, run the installation.

Once we have installed both Vagrant and VirtualBox, starting a base VM is as simple as typing the following lines in the terminal or command prompt depending on the OS you use:

```
$ vagrant box add lucid32 http://files.vagrantup.com/lucid32.box
$ vagrant init lucid32
$ vagrant up
```

These commands will start a new Vagrant box with Ubuntu Linux installed. From this point onward, we could start installing our LAMP as normal. But why should we spend an hour to configure and set up a LAMP server for each project when we can use Chef to automatically do it? Chef is a configuration management tool written in Ruby that integrates into Vagrant.

To make it easier for developers who start working with Magento, I have created a Vagrant repository on Github called `magento-vagrant` that includes all the necessary cookbooks and recipes for Chef. The `magento-vagrant` repository also includes a new cookbook that will take care of the specific Magento setup and configuration.

In order to start working with `magento-vagrant`, you will need a working copy of Git.

If you are using Ubuntu, run the following command:

```
$ sudo apt-get install git-core -y
```

For Windows, we can use the native tool at `http://windows.github.com/` to download and manage our repositories.

Regardless of the operating system that you are using, we will need to check out a copy of this repository into our local filesystem. We will use `C:/Users/magedev/Documents/magento-vagrant/` to download and save our repository; inside `magento-vagrant` we will find the following files and directories:

- `cookbooks`
- `data_bags`

- Public
- .vagrant
- Vagrantfile

The `magento-vagrant` repository includes cookbooks for each of the components of our development environment, which will be installed automatically as soon as we start our new Vagrant box.

The only thing now left to do is to set up our development sites. The process of adding new Magento sites to our Vagrant installation has been simplified through the use of Vagrant and Chef.

Inside the `data_bags` directory, we have one file for each Magento installation inside our Vagrant box; the default repository comes with an example installation of Magento CE 1.7.

For each site, we will need to create a new JSON file containing all the settings that Chef will need. Let's take a look at the `magento-vagrant` default file, which can be found at the location `C:/Users/magedev/Documents/magento-vagrant/data_bags/sites/default.json`:

```
{
    "id": "default",
    "host": "magento.localhost.com",
    "repo": [
        "url": "svn.magentocommerce.com/source/branches/1.7",
        "revision": "HEAD"
    ],
    "database": [
      "name": "magento_staging",
      "username": "magento",
      "password": "magento2013$"
    ]
}
```

This will automatically set up a Magento installation using the latest files from the Magento repository.

Adding new sites to our Vagrant box is just a matter of adding a new JSON file for the corresponding site and restarting the Vagrant box.

Now that we have a running Magento installation, let's look into choosing a proper **integrated development environment (IDE)**.

Choosing an IDE

Choosing the right IDE is mostly a matter of a personal developer's taste. However, choosing the right IDE can be critical for a Magento developer.

The challenge for the IDEs comes mostly from Magento's extensive usage of factory names. This makes the implementation of certain features such as code completion (also known as intellisense) difficult. Currently, there are two IDEs that excel on their native support of Magento – NetBeans and PhpStorm.

Although NetBeans is open source and has been around for a long time, PhpStorm has been taking the upper hand and gaining more support from the Magento community.

Furthermore, a recent release of Magicento, a plugin specifically created to extend and integrate Magento into PhpStorm, has made it the best option among currently available options.

Working with a version control system

The Magento code base is very extensive, comprising of over 7,000 files and close to a million and half lines of code. For this reason, working with a version control system is not only a good practice but also a necessity.

Version control systems are used to keep track of changes across multiple files and by multiple developers; by using a version control system we gain access to very powerful tools.

Of the several version control systems available (Git, SVN, Mercurial), Git deserves special attention due to its simplicity and flexibility. By releasing the upcoming version 2 of Magento on Github, a Git hosting service, the Magento core development team has recognized the importance that Git has among the Magento community.

For more information on Magento2, please visit https://github.com/magento/magento2.

Github now includes a .gitignore file specifically for Magento, which will ignore all the files in the Magento core and only keep track of our own code.

That said, there are several version control concepts that we need to keep in mind when working with our Magento projects:

- **Branching**: This allows us to work on new features without affecting our trunk (stable release).
- **Merging**: This is used to move code from one place to another. Usually, this is done from a development brand to our trunk once the code is ready to be moved into production.
- **Tagging**: This is used for creating snapshots of a release.

Summary

In this first chapter, we learned about setting up and working with LAMP environments, setting development environments across multiple platforms, creating and provisioning Vagrant virtual machines, working with Chef recipes, and using version control systems for Magento development.

Having a proper environment is the first step for starting developing for Magento, and it is an integral part of our Magento toolbox.

Now that we have a development environment set up and ready to use, it is time to dive deep into the Magento fundamental concepts; these concepts will give us the necessary tools and knowledge for developing with Magento.

2
Magento Fundamentals for Developers

In this chapter, we will cover the fundamental concepts for working with Magento. We will learn how Magento is structured, and we will go over the source of Magento's flexibility, that is, its modular architecture.

Magento is a flexible and powerful system. Unfortunately, this adds some level of complexity too. Currently, a clean installation of Magento has around 30,000 files and over 1.2 million lines of code.

With all that power and complexity, Magento can be daunting for new developers; but don't worry. This chapter is designed to teach new developers all the fundamental concepts and tools they will need to use and extend Magento, and in the next chapter, we will be diving deep into Magento models and data collections.

Zend Framework – the base of Magento

As you probably know, Magento is the most powerful e-commerce platform in the market; what you might not know about Magento is that it is also an **object-oriented** (**OO**) PHP framework developed on top of Zend Framework.

Zend's official site describes the framework as:

> *Zend Framework 2 is an open source framework for developing web applications and services using PHP 5.3+. Zend Framework 2 uses 100% object-oriented code and utilises most of the new features of PHP 5.3, namely namespaces, late static binding, lambda functions and closures.*

The component structure of Zend Framework 2 is unique; each component is designed with few dependencies on other components. ZF2 follows the SOLID object oriented design principle. This loosely coupled architecture allows developers to use whichever components they want. We call this a "use-at-will" design.

But what is Zend Framework exactly? Zend Framework is an OO framework developed on PHP that implements the **Model-View-Controller** (**MVC**) paradigm. When Varien, now Magento Inc., started developing Magento it decided to do it on top of Zend because of the following components:

- `Zend_Cache`
- `Zend_Acl`
- `Zend_Locale`
- `Zend_DB`
- `Zend_Pdf`
- `Zend_Currency`
- `Zend_Date`
- `Zend_Soap`
- `Zend_Http`

In total, Magento uses around 15 different Zend components. The Varien library directly extends several of the Zend components mentioned previously, for example `Varien_Cache_Core` extends from `Zend_Cache_Core`.

Using Zend Framework, Magento was built with the following principles in mind:

- **Maintainability**: It occurs using code pools to keep the core code separate from local customizations and third-party modules
- **Upgradability**: Magento modularity allows extensions and third-party modules to be updated independently from the rest of the system
- **Flexibility**: Allows seamless customization and simplifies the development of new features

Although having used Zend Framework or even understanding it are not the requirements for developing with Magento, having at least a basic understanding of the Zend components, usage, and interaction can be invaluable information when we start digging deeper into the core of Magento.

 You can learn more about Zend Framework at `http://framework.zend.com/`.

Magento folder structure

Magento folder structure is slightly different from other MVC applications; let's take a look at the directory tree, and each directory and its functions:

- `app`: This folder is the core of Magento and is subdivided into three importing directories:
    - ° `code`: This contains all our application code divided into three code pools such as `core`, `community`, and `local`
    - ° `design`: This contains all the templates and layouts for our application
    - ° `locale`: This contains all the translation and e-mail template files used for the store

- `js`: This contains all the JavaScript libraries that are used in Magento

- `media`: This contains all the images and media files for our products and CMS pages as well as the product image cache

- `lib`: This contains all the third-party libraries used in Magento such as Zend and PEAR, as well as the custom libraries developed by Magento, which reside under the Varien and Mage directories

- `skin`: This contains all CSS code, images, and JavaScript files used by the corresponding theme

- `var`: This contains our temporary data such as cache files, index lock files, sessions, import/export files, and in the case of the Enterprise edition the full page cache folders

Magento is a modular system. This means that the application, including the core, is divided into smaller modules. For this reason, the folder structure plays a key role in the organization of each module core; a typical Magento module folder structure would look something like the following figure:

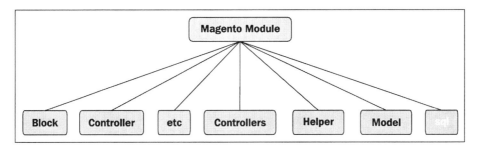

Let's review each folder in more detail:

- `Block`: This folder contains blocks in Magento that form an additional layer of logic between the controllers and views
- `controllers`: `controllers` folders are formed by actions that process web server requests
- `Controller`: The classes in this folder are meant to be abstract classes and extended by the `controller` class under the the `controllers` folder
- `etc`: Here we can find the module-specific configuration in the form of XML files such as `config.xml` and `system.xml`
- `Helper`: This folder contains auxiliary classes that encapsulate a common-module functionality and make it available to a class of the same module and to other modules' classes as well
- `Model`: This folder contains models that support the controllers in the module for interacting with data
- `sql`: This folder contains the installation and upgrade files for each specific module

As we will see later on in this chapter, Magento makes heavy use of factory names and factory methods. This is why the folder structure is so important.

Modular architecture

Rather than being a large application, Magento is built by smaller modules, each adding specific functionality to Magento.

One of the advantages of this approach is the ability to enable and disable specific module functionality with ease, as well as add new functionality by adding new modules.

Autoloader

Magento is a huge framework, composed of close to 30,000 files. Requiring every single file when the application starts would make it incredibly slow and heavy. For this reason, Magento makes use of an autoloader class to find the required files each time a factory method is called.

So, what exactly is an autoloader? PHP5 includes a function called `__autoload()`. When instantiating a class, the `__autoload()` function is automatically called; inside this function, custom logic is defined to parse the class name and the required file.

Let's take a closer look at the Magento bootstrap code located at `app/Mage.php`:

```
...
Mage::register('original_include_path', get_include_path());
if (defined('COMPILER_INCLUDE_PATH')) {
    $appPath = COMPILER_INCLUDE_PATH;
    set_include_path($appPath . PS .
    Mage::registry('original_include_path'));
    include_once "Mage_Core_functions.php";
    include_once "Varien_Autoload.php";
} else {
    /**
     * Set include path
     */
    $paths[] = BP . DS . 'app' . DS . 'code' . DS . 'local';
    $paths[] = BP . DS . 'app' . DS . 'code' . DS . 'community';
    $paths[] = BP . DS . 'app' . DS . 'code' . DS . 'core';
    $paths[] = BP . DS . 'lib';

    $appPath = implode(PS, $paths);
    set_include_path($appPath . PS .
    Mage::registry('original_include_path'));
    include_once "Mage/Core/functions.php";
    include_once "Varien/Autoload.php";
}

Varien_Autoload::register();
```

The bootstrap file takes care of defining the `include` paths and initializing the Varien autoloader, which will in turn define its own `autoload` function as the default function to call. Let's take a look under the hood and see what the Varien `autoload` function is doing:

```
    /**
     * Load class source code
     *
     * @param string $class
     */
    public function autoload($class)
    {
        if ($this->_collectClasses) {
            $this->_arrLoadedClasses[self::$_scope][] = $class;
        }
        if ($this->_isIncludePathDefined) {
```

```
        $classFile =  COMPILER_INCLUDE_PATH .
        DIRECTORY_SEPARATOR . $class;
    } else {
        $classFile = str_replace(' ', DIRECTORY_SEPARATOR,
        ucwords(str_replace('_', ' ', $class)));
    }
    $classFile.= '.php';
    //echo $classFile;die();
    return include $classFile;
}
```

The `autoload` class takes a single parameter called `$class`, which is an alias provided by the factory method. This alias is processed to generate a matching class name that is then included.

As we mentioned before, Magento's directory structure is important due to the fact that Magento derives its class names from the directory structure. This convention is the core principle behind factory methods that we will be reviewing later on in this chapter.

Code pools

As we mentioned before, inside our `app/code` folder we have our application code divided into three different directories known as code pools. They are as follows:

- `core`: This is where the Magento core modules that provide the base functionality reside. The golden rule among Magento developers is that you should never, by any circumstance, modify any files under the `core` code pool.

- `community`: This is the location where third-party modules are placed. They are either provided by third parties or installed through Magento Connect.

- `local`: This is where all the modules and code developed specifically for this instance of Magento reside.

The code pools identify where the module came from and on which order they should be loaded. If we take another look at the `Mage.php` bootstrap file, we can see the order on which code pools are loaded:

```
$paths[] = BP . DS . 'app' . DS . 'code' . DS . 'local';
$paths[] = BP . DS . 'app' . DS . 'code' . DS . 'community';
$paths[] = BP . DS . 'app' . DS . 'code' . DS . 'core';
$paths[] = BP . DS . 'lib';
```

This means that for each class request, Magento will look in `local`, then `community`, then `core`, and finally inside the `lib` folder.

This also leads to an interesting behavior that can easily be used for overriding `core` and `community` classes, by just copying the directory structure and matching the class name.

 Needless to say that this is a terrible practice, but it is still useful to know about just in case you someday have to take care of a project that exploits this behavior.

Routing and request flow

Before going into more detail about the different components that form a part of Magento, it is important that we understand how these components interact together and how Magento processes requests coming from the web server.

As with any other PHP application, we have a single file as an entry point for every request; in the case of Magento this file is `index.php`, which is in charge of loading the `Mage.php` bootstrap class and starting the request cycle. It then goes through the following steps:

1. The web server receives the request and Magento is instantiated by calling the bootstrap file, `Mage.php`.

2. The frontend controller is instantiated and initialized; during this controller initialization Magento searches for the web routes and instantiates them.

3. Magento then iterates through each of the routers and calls the match. The `match` method is responsible for processing the URL and generating the corresponding controller and action.

4. Magento then instantiates the matching controller and takes the corresponding action.

Routers are especially important in this process. The `Router` objects are used by the frontend controller to match a requested URL (route) to a module controller and action. By default, Magento comes with the following routers:

- `Mage_Core_Controller_Varien_Router_Admin`
- `Mage_Core_Controller_Varien_Router_Standard`
- `Mage_Core_Controller_Varien_Router_Default`

The action controller will then load and render the layout, which in turn will load the corresponding blocks, models, and templates.

Let's analyze how Magento will handle a request to a category page; we will use `http://localhost/catalog/category/view/id/10` as an example. Magento URIs are comprised of three parts – */FrontName/ControllerName/ActionName*.

This means that for our example URL, the breakdown would be as follows:

- **FrontName**: `catalog`
- **ControllerName**: `category`
- **ActionName**: `view`

If I take a look at the Magento router class, I can see the `Mage_Core_Controller_Varien_Router_Standard` match function:

```
public function match(Zend_Controller_Request_Http $request)
{
    ...
    $path = trim($request->getPathInfo(), '/');
            if ($path) {
                $p = explode('/', $path);
            } else {
                $p = explode('/', $this->_getDefaultPath());
            }
    ...
}
```

From the preceding code, we can see that the first thing the router tries to do is to parse the URI into an array. Based on our example URL, the corresponding array would be something like the following code snippet:

```
$p = Array
(
    [0] => catalog
    [1] => category
    [2] => view
)
```

The next part of the function will first try to check if the request has the module name specified; if not, then it tries to determine the module name based on the first element of our array. And if a module name can't be provided, then the function will return `false`. Let's take a look at that part of the code:

```
// get module name
  if ($request->getModuleName()) {
      $module = $request->getModuleName();
  } else {
```

```
            if (!empty($p[0])) {
                $module = $p[0];
            } else {
                $module = $this->getFront()->getDefault('module');
                $request->setAlias(Mage_Core_Model_Url_Rewrite::
                REWRITE_REQUEST_PATH_ALIAS, '');
            }
        }
        if (!$module) {
            if (Mage::app()->getStore()->isAdmin()) {
                $module = 'admin';
            } else {
                return false;
            }
        }
    }
```

Next, the match function will iterate through each of the available modules and try
to match the controller and action, using the following code:

```
    ...
        foreach ($modules as $realModule) {
            $request->setRouteName
            ($this->getRouteByFrontName($module));

            // get controller name
            if ($request->getControllerName()) {
                $controller = $request->getControllerName();
            } else {
                if (!empty($p[1])) {
                    $controller = $p[1];
                } else {
                    $controller =
                    $front->getDefault('controller');
                    $request->setAlias(
                        Mage_Core_Model_Url_Rewrite::REWRITE_REQUEST_
PATH_ALIAS,
                        ltrim($request->
                        getOriginalPathInfo(), '/')
                    );
                }
            }

            // get action name
            if (empty($action)) {
                if ($request->getActionName()) {
```

```
                    $action = $request->getActionName();
            } else {
                $action = !empty($p[2]) ? $p[2] :
                $front->getDefault('action');
            }
        }

        //checking if this place should be secure
        $this->_checkShouldBeSecure($request,
        '/'.$module.'/'.$controller.'/'.$action);

        $controllerClassName = $this->_validate
        ControllerClassName($realModule, $controller);
        if (!$controllerClassName) {
            continue;
        }

        // instantiate controller class
        $controllerInstance = Mage::getControllerInstance
        ($controllerClassName,
        $request, $front->getResponse());

        if (!$controllerInstance->hasAction($action)) {
            continue;
        }

        $found = true;
        break;
    }
...
```

Now that looks like an awful lot of code, so let's break it down even further. The first part of the loop will check if the request has a controller name; if it is not set, it will check our parameter array's ($p) second value and try to determine the controller name, and then it will try to do the same for the action name.

If we got this far in the loop, we should have a module name, a controller name, and an action name, which Magento will now use to try and get a matching controller class name by calling the following function:

```
$controllerClassName = $this->_validateControllerClassName($realModu
le, $controller);
```

This function will not only generate a matching class name but it will also validate its existence; in our example case this function should return Mage_Catalog_ CategoryController.

Since we now have a valid class name, we can proceed to instantiate our controller object; if you were paying attention up to this point, you have probably noticed that we haven't done anything with our action yet, and that's precisely the next step in our loop.

Our new instantiated controller comes with a very handy function called `hasAction()`; in essence, what this function does is to call a PHP function called `is_callable()`, which will check if our current controller has a public function matching the action name; in our case this will be `viewAction()`.

The reason behind this elaborate matching process and the use of a `foreach` loop is that it is possible for several modules to use the same FrontName.

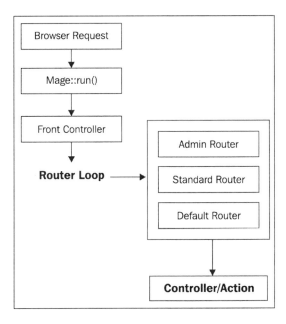

Now, `http://localhost/catalog/category/view/id/10` is not a very user-friendly URL; fortunately, Magento has its own URL rewrite system that allows us to use `http://localhost/books.html`.

Let's dig a little deeper into the URL rewrite system and see how Magento gets the controller and action names from our URL alias. Inside our `Varien/Front.php` controller dispatch function, Magento will call:

```
Mage::getModel('core/url_rewrite')->rewrite();
```

Before actually looking into the inner workings of the `rewrite` function, let's take a look at the structure of the `core/url_rewrite` model:

```
Array (
   ["url_rewrite_id"] => "10"
   ["store_id"]       => "1"
   ["category_id"]    => "10"
   ["product_id"]     => NULL
   ["id_path"]        => "category/10"
   ["request_path"]   => "books.html"
   ["target_path"]    => "catalog/category/view/id/10"
   ["is_system"]      => "1"
   ["options"]        => NULL
   ["description"]    => NULL
)
```

As we can see, the rewrite module is comprised of several properties, but only two of them are of particular interest to use – `request_path` and `target_path`. Simply put, the job of the rewrite module is to modify the request object path information with the matching values of `target_path`.

Magento version of MVC

If you are familiar with the traditional MVC implementations such as CakePHP or Symfony, you may know that the most common implementation is called a convention-based MVC. With a convention-based MVC, to add a new model or let's say a controller, you only need to create the file/class (following the framework conventions) and the system will pick it up automatically.

Magento, on the other hand, uses a configuration-based MVC pattern, meaning that creating our file/class is not enough; we explicitly have to tell Magento that we added a new class.

Each Magento module has a `config.xml` file, which is located under the module `etc/` directory and contains all the relevant module configuration. For example, if we want to add a new module that includes a new model, we would need to define a node in the configuration file that tells Magento where to find our model, such as:

```
<global>
...
<models>
    <group_classname>
        <class>Namespace_Modulename_Model</class>
    <group_classname>
```

```
    </models>
    ...
    </global>
```

Although this might look like additional work, it also gives us a huge amount of flexibility and power. For example, we can rewrite another class by using the `rewrite` node:

```
<global>
...
<models>
    <group_classname>
     <rewrite>
            <modulename>Namespace_Modulename_Model</modulename>
     </rewrite>
    <group_classname>
</models>
...
</global>
```

Magento will then load all the `config.xml` files and merge them at runtime, creating a single configuration tree.

Additionally, modules can also have a `system.xml` file, which is used to specify configuration options in the Magento backend, which in turn can be used by end users to configure the module functionality. A snippet of a `system.xml` file would look like the following code:

```
<config>
  <sections>
    <section_name translate="label">
      <label>Section Description</label>
      <tab>general</tab>
      <frontend_type>text</frontend_type>
      <sort_order>1000</sort_order>
      <show_in_default>1</show_in_default>
      <show_in_website>1</show_in_website>
      <show_in_store>1</show_in_store>
      <groups>
       <group_name translate="label">
         <label>Demo Of Config Fields</label>
         <frontend_type>text</frontend_type>
         <sort_order>1</sort_order>
         <show_in_default>1</show_in_default>
         <show_in_website>1</show_in_website>
```

```
                    <show_in_store>1</show_in_store>
        <fields>
                <field_name translate="label comment">
                    <label>Enabled</label>
                    <comment>
                      <![CDATA[Comments can contain
                      <strong>HTML</strong>]]>
                    </comment>
                    <frontend_type>select</frontend_type>
                    <source_model>adminhtml/system_config_source_yesno</
source_model>
                    <sort_order>10</sort_order>
                    <show_in_default>1</show_in_default>
                    <show_in_website>1</show_in_website>
                    <show_in_store>1</show_in_store>
                </field_name>
            </fields>
          </group_name>
        </groups>
      </section_name>
    </sections>
</config>
```

Let's break down each node function:

- `section_name`: This is just an arbitrary name that we use to identify our configuration section; inside this node we will specify all the fields and groups for the configuration section.

- `group`: Groups, as the name implies, are used to group configuration options and display them inside an accordion section.

- `label`: This defines the title or label to be used on the field/section/group.

- `tab`: This defines the tab on which the section should be displayed.

- `frontend_type`: This node allows us to specify which render to use for our custom option field. Some of the available options are:
    - button
    - checkboxes
    - checkbox
    - date

- ○ file
- ○ hidden
- ○ image
- ○ label
- ○ link
- ○ multiline
- ○ multiselect
- ○ password
- ○ radio
- ○ radios
- ○ select
- ○ submit
- ○ textarea
- ○ text
- ○ time

- sort_order: It specifies the position of the field, group, or section.
- source_model: Certain type of fields such as a select field can take options from a source model. Magento already provides several useful classes under Mage/Adminhtml/Model/System/Config/Source. Some of the classes we can find are:
  - ○ YesNo
  - ○ Country
  - ○ Currency
  - ○ AllRegions
  - ○ Category
  - ○ Language

By just using XML, we can build complex configuration options for our modules right on the Magento backend, without having to worry about setting up templates for populating fields or validating data.

Magento is also kind enough to provide a comprehensive amount of form field validation models, which we can use with the `<validate>` tag. Among the following field validators we have:

- `validate-email`
- `validate-length`
- `validate-url`
- `validate-select`
- `validate-password`

As with any other part of Magento we can extend the `source_model`, `frontend_type`, and `validator` functions and even create new ones. We will be tackling this task in a later chapter where we will create a new type of each. But for now, we will explore the concepts of models, views, file layouts, and controllers.

Models

Magento makes use of the ORM approach; although we can still use `Zend_Db` to access the database directly, we will be using models to access our data most of the time. For this type of task, Magento provides the following two types of models:

- **Simple models**: This model implementations are a simple mapping of one object to one table, meaning our object attributes match each field and our table structure
- **Entity Attribute Value (EAV) models**: This type of models are used to describe entities with a dynamic number of attributes

Magento splits the model layer up into two parts: a model handling the business logic and a resource handling the database interaction. This design decision allows Magento to eventually support multiple database platforms without having to change any of the logic inside the models.

Magento ORM uses one of PHP's magic class methods to provide dynamic access to object properties. In the next chapter we will look into models, the Magento ORM, and the data collections in more detail.

 Magento models don't necessarily have to be related to any type of table in the database or an EAV entity. Observers, who we will be reviewing later, are perfect examples of this type of Magento models.

Views

The view layer is one of the areas where Magento truly sets itself apart from other MVC applications. Unlike traditional MVC systems, Magento's view layer is divided into the following three different components:

- **Layouts**: Layouts are XML files that define the block structure and properties such as name and the template file we can use. Each Magento module has its own set of layout files.

- **Blocks**: Blocks are used in Magento to reduce the burden on the controller by moving most of the logic into blocks.

- **Templates**: Templates are PHTML files that contain the required HTML code and PHP tags.

Layouts give the Magento frontend an amazing amount of flexibility. Each module has its own layout XML files, which tell Magento what to include and render on each page request. Through the use of the layouts, we can move, add, or remove blocks from our store without worrying about changing anything else other than our XML files.

Dissecting a layout file

Let's examine one of the core layout files of Magento, in this case `catalog.xml`:

```xml
<layout version="0.1.0">
<default>
    <reference name="left">
        <block type="core/template" name="left.permanent.callout"
        template="callouts/left_col.phtml">
            <action method="setImgSrc">
            <src>images/media/col_left_callout.jpg</src></action>
            <action method="setImgAlt" translate="alt"
            module="catalog"><alt>
            Our customer service is available 24/7.
            Call us at (555) 555-0123.</alt></action>
            <action method="setLinkUrl">
            <url>checkout/cart</url></action>
        </block>
    </reference>
    <reference name="right">
        <block type="catalog/product_compare_sidebar"
        before="cart_sidebar" name="catalog.compare.sidebar"
        template="catalog/product/compare/sidebar.phtml"/>
        <block type="core/template" name="right.permanent.callout"
        template="callouts/right_col.phtml">
```

```
            <action method="setImgSrc">
            <src>images/media/col_right_callout.jpg</src></action>
            <action method="setImgAlt" translate="alt"
            module="catalog"><alt>
            Visit our site and save A LOT!</alt></action>
        </block>
    </reference>
    <reference name="footer_links">
        <action method="addLink" translate="label title"
        module="catalog" ifconfig="catalog/seo/site_map">
        <label>Site Map</label><url
        helper="catalog/map/getCategoryUrl" />
        <title>Site Map</title></action>
    </reference>
    <block type="catalog/product_price_template"
    name="catalog_product_price_template" />
</default>
```

Layout blocks are comprised of three main XML nodes, as follows:

- `handle`: Each page request will have several unique handles; the layout uses these handles to tell Magento which blocks to load and render on a per page basis. The most commonly used handles are `default` and `[frontname]_[controller]_[action]`.

  The `default` handle is especially useful for setting global blocks, for example adding a CSS or JavaScript to all pages on the header block.

- `reference`: A `<reference>` node is used to make references to a block. It is useful for specifying nested blocks or modifying an already existing block. In our example we can see a new children block being specified inside `<reference name="left">`.

- `block`: The `<block>` node is used to load our actual blocks. Each block node can have the following properties:

  - `type`: This is the identifier for the actual block class. For example, `catalog/product_list` makes reference to the `Mage_Catalog_Block_Product_List`.

  - `name`: This is the name used by other blocks to make reference to this block.

  - `before/after`: These properties can be used to position the blocks relative to other blocks' position. Both these properties can use a hyphen as a value to specify if the module should appear at the very top or the very bottom.

- ° `template`: This property determines the `.phtml` template file, which will be used for rendering the block.

- ° `action`: Each block type has specific actions that affect the frontend functionality. For instance, the `page/html_head` block, which has actions for adding CSS and JavaScript (`addJs` and `addCss`).

- ° `as`: This is used to specify the unique identifier that we will be using for calling the block from the template, for example calling a child block by using `getChildHtml('block_name')`.

Blocks are a new concept that Magento implements in order to reduce the controller load. They are basically data resources that communicate directly with the models, which manipulate the data, if needed, and then pass it to the views.

Finally, we have our PHTML files; the templates contain the `html` and `php` tags and are in charge of formatting and displaying the data from our models. Let's take a look at a snippet from the product view template:

```
<div class="product-view">
...
    <div class="product-name">
        <h1><?php echo $_helper->productAttribute
        ($_product, $_product->getName(), 'name') ?></h1>
    </div>
...
    <?php echo $this->getReviewsSummaryHtml
    ($_product, false, true)?>
    <?php echo $this->getChildHtml('alert_urls') ?>
    <?php echo $this->getChildHtml('product_type_data') ?>
    <?php echo $this->getTierPriceHtml() ?>
    <?php echo $this->getChildHtml('extrahint') ?>
...

    <?php if ($_product->getShortDescription()):?>
        <div class="short-description">
            <h2><?php echo $this->__('Quick Overview') ?></h2>
            <div class="std"><?php echo $_helper->
            productAttribute($_product, nl2br($_product->
            getShortDescription()), 'short_description') ?></div>
        </div>
    <?php endif;?>
...
</div>
```

The following is the block diagram of MVC:

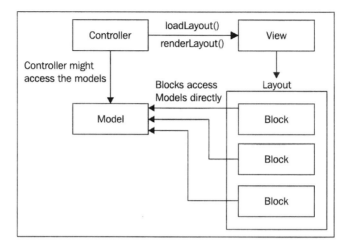

Controllers

In Magento, MVC controllers are designed to be thin controllers; thin controllers have little business logic and are mostly used for driving the application requests. A basic Magento controller action would just load and render the layout:

```
public function viewAction()
{
    $this->loadLayout();
    $this->renderLayout();
}
```

From here it is the job of the blocks to handle the display logic, get the data from our models, prepare the data, and send it to the views.

Websites and store scopes

One of the core features of Magento is the ability to handle multiple websites and stores with a single Magento installation; internally, Magento refers to each of these instances as scopes.

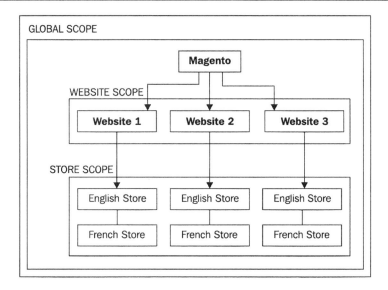

Values for certain elements such as products, categories, attributes, and configurations are scope specific and can differ on different scopes; this gives Magento tremendous flexibility, for example, a product can be set up on two different websites with different prices but can still share the rest of the attribute configuration.

As developers, one of the areas where we will be using scopes the most is when working with configuration. The different configuration scopes available in Magento are:

- **Global**: As the name implies, this applies across all scopes.
- **Website**: These are defined by a domain name and are composed by one or more stores. Websites can be set up to share customer data or be completely isolated.
- **Store**: Stores are used to manage products and categories, and to group store views. Stores also have a root category that allows us to have separated catalogs per store.
- **Store view**: By using store views we can set up multiple languages on our store frontend.

Configuration options in Magento can store values on three scopes (global, website, and store view); by default, all the values are set on the global scope. By using `system.xml` on our modules, we can specify the scopes on which the configuration options can be set; let's revisit our previous `system.xml`:

```
...
<field_name translate="label comment">
    <label>Enabled</label>
    <comment>
        <![CDATA[Comments can contain <strong>HTML</strong>]]>
    </comment>
    <frontend_type>select</frontend_type>
    <source_model>adminhtml/system_config_source_yesno</source_model>
    <sort_order>10</sort_order>
    <show_in_default>1</show_in_default>
    <show_in_website>1</show_in_website>
    <show_in_store>1</show_in_store>
</field_name>
...
```

Factory names and functions

Magento makes use of factory methods to instantiate `Model`, `Helper`, and `Block` classes. A factory method is a design pattern that allows us to instantiate an object without using the exact class name and using a class alias instead.

Magento implements several factory methods, as follows:

- `Mage::getModel()`
- `Mage::getResourceModel()`
- `Mage::helper()`
- `Mage::getSingleton()`
- `Mage::getResourceSingleton()`
- `Mage::getResourceHelper()`

Each of these methods takes a class alias that is used to determine the real class name of the object that we are trying to instantiate; for example, if we wanted to instantiate a `product` object, we can do so by calling the `getModel()` method:

```
$product = Mage::getModel('catalog/product');
```

Notice that we are passing a factory name composed of group_classname/model_ name; Magento will resolve this to the actual class name of Mage_Catalog_Model_ Product. Let's take a closer look at the inner workings of getModel():

```
public static function getModel($modelClass = '', $arguments =
array())
    {
        return self::getConfig()->getModelInstance
        ($modelClass, $arguments);
    }
```

getModel calls the getModelInstance from the Mage_Core_Model_Config class.

```
public function getModelInstance($modelClass='',
$constructArguments=array())
{
    $className = $this->getModelClassName($modelClass);
    if (class_exists($className)) {
        Varien_Profiler::start('CORE::create_object_of::'.$className);
        $obj = new $className($constructArguments);
        Varien_Profiler::stop('CORE::create_object_of::'.$className);
        return $obj;
    } else {
        return false;
    }
}
```

getModelInstance() in return calls the getModelClassName() method, which takes our class alias as a parameter. Then it tries to validate the existence of the returned class, and if the class exists, it will create a new instance of that class and return it to our getModel() method:

```
public function getModelClassName($modelClass)
{
    $modelClass = trim($modelClass);
    if (strpos($modelClass, '/')===false) {
        return $modelClass;
    }
    return $this->getGroupedClassName('model', $modelClass);
}
```

getModelClassName() calls the getGroupedClassName() method, which is actually in charge of returning the real class name of our model.

getGroupedClassName() takes two parameters – $groupType and $classId; $groupType refers to the type of object that we are trying to instantiate (currently only models, blocks, and helpers are supported) and $classId, which we are trying to instantiate.

```
public function getGroupedClassName($groupType, $classId,
$groupRootNode=null)
{
    if (empty($groupRootNode)) {
        $groupRootNode = 'global/'.$groupType.'s';
    }
    $classArr = explode('/', trim($classId));
    $group = $classArr[0];
    $class = !empty($classArr[1]) ? $classArr[1] : null;

    if (isset($this->_classNameCache
    [$groupRootNode][$group][$class])) {
        return $this->_classNameCache
        [$groupRootNode][$group][$class];
    }
    $config = $this->_xml->global->{$groupType.'s'}->{$group};
    $className = null;
    if (isset($config->rewrite->$class)) {
        $className = (string)$config->rewrite->$class;
    } else {
        if ($config->deprecatedNode) {
            $deprecatedNode = $config->deprecatedNode;
            $configOld = $this->_xml->global->
            {$groupType.'s'}->$deprecatedNode;
            if (isset($configOld->rewrite->$class)) {
                $className = (string) $configOld->rewrite->$class;
            }
        }
    }
    if (empty($className)) {
        if (!empty($config)) {
            $className = $config->getClassName();
        }
        if (empty($className)) {
            $className = 'mage_'.$group.'_'.$groupType;
        }
        if (!empty($class)) {
```

```
            $className .= '_'.$class;
        }
        $className = uc_words($className);
    }
    $this->_classNameCache
    [$groupRootNode][$group][$class] = $className;
    return $className;
}
```

As we can see, `getGroupedClassName()` is actually doing all the work; it grabs our class alias `catalog/product` and creates an array by exploding the string on the slash character.

Then, it loads an instance of `VarienSimplexml_Element` and passes the first value in our array (`group_classname`). It will also check if the class has been rewritten, and if it has, we will use the corresponding group name.

Magento also uses a custom version of the `uc_words()` function, which will capitalize the first letters and convert separators of the class alias if needed.

Finally, the function will return the real class name to the `getModelInstance()` function; in our example case it will return `Mage_Catalog_Model_Product`.

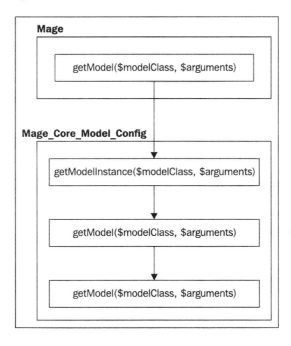

Events and observers

The event and observer pattern is probably one of Magento's more interesting features, since it allows developers to extend Magento in critical parts of the application flow.

In order to provide more flexibility and facilitate the interaction between the different modules, Magento implements an event/observer pattern; this pattern allows for modules to be loosely coupled.

There are two parts of this system – an event dispatch with the object and event information, and an observer listening to a particular event.

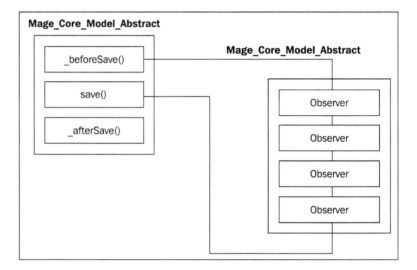

Event dispatch

Events are created or dispatched using the `Mage::dispatchEvent()` function. The core team has already created several events on critical parts of the core. For example, the model abstract class `Mage_Core_Model_Abstract` calls two protected functions every time a model is saved – `_beforeSave()` and `_afterSave()`; on each of these methods two events are fired:

```
protected function _beforeSave()
{
    if (!$this->getId()) {
        $this->isObjectNew(true);
    }
    Mage::dispatchEvent('model_save_before',
    array('object'=>$this));
```

```
    Mage::dispatchEvent($this->_eventPrefix.'_save_before',
    $this->_getEventData());
    return $this;
}

protected function _afterSave()
{
    $this->cleanModelCache();
    Mage::dispatchEvent('model_save_after',
    array('object'=>$this));
    Mage::dispatchEvent($this->_eventPrefix.'_save_after',
    $this->_getEventData());
    return $this;
}
```

Each function fires a generic `mode_save_after` event, and then a dynamic version based on the type of object being saved. This gives us a wide range of possibilities for manipulating objects through observers.

The `Mage::dispatchEvent()` method takes two parameters: the first is the event name and the second is an array of data that is received by the observer. We can pass values or objects in this array. This comes in handy if we want to manipulate the objects.

In order to understand the details of the event system, let's take a look at the `dispatchEvent()` method:

```
public static function dispatchEvent($name, array $data = array())
{
    $result = self::app()->dispatchEvent($name, $data);
    return $result;
}
```

This function is actually an alias to the `dispatchEvent()` function inside the `app` core class located in `Mage_Core_Model_App`:

```
public function dispatchEvent($eventName, $args)
{
    foreach ($this->_events as $area=>$events) {
        if (!isset($events[$eventName])) {
            $eventConfig = $this->getConfig()->
            getEventConfig($area, $eventName);
            if (!$eventConfig) {
                $this->_events[$area][$eventName] = false;
                continue;
            }
```

```
        $observers = array();
        foreach ($eventConfig->observers->
        children() as $obsName=>$obsConfig) {
            $observers[$obsName] = array(
                'type'  => (string)$obsConfig->type,
                'model' => $obsConfig->class ?
                (string)$obsConfig->
                class : $obsConfig->getClassName(),
                'method'=> (string)$obsConfig->method,
                'args'  => (array)$obsConfig->args,
            );
        }
        $events[$eventName]['observers'] = $observers;
        $this->_events
        [$area][$eventName]['observers'] = $observers;
    }
    if (false===$events[$eventName]) {
        continue;
    } else {
        $event = new Varien_Event($args);
        $event->setName($eventName);
        $observer = new Varien_Event_Observer();
    }

    foreach ($events[$eventName]
    ['observers'] as $obsName=>$obs) {
        $observer->setData(array('event'=>$event));
        Varien_Profiler::start('OBSERVER: '.$obsName);
        switch ($obs['type']) {
            case 'disabled':
                break;
            case 'object':
            case 'model':
                $method = $obs['method'];
                $observer->addData($args);
                $object = Mage::getModel($obs['model']);
                $this->_callObserverMethod
                ($object, $method, $observer);
                break;
            default:
                $method = $obs['method'];
                $observer->addData($args);
                $object = Mage::getSingleton($obs['model']);
                $this->_callObserverMethod
                ($object, $method, $observer);
```

```
                 break;
         }
         Varien_Profiler::stop('OBSERVER: '.$obsName);
      }
   }
   return $this;
}
```

The `dispatchEvent()` method is actually doing all the work on the event/observer model:

1. It gets the Magento configuration object.
2. It walks through the observer's node children, checking if the defined observer is listening to the current event.
3. For each of the available observers, the dispatch event will try to instantiate the observer object.
4. Lastly, Magento will try to call the corresponding observer function mapped to this particular event.

Observer bindings

Now, dispatching an event is the only part of the equation. We also need to tell Magento which observer is listening to each event. Not to our surprise, observers are specified through `config.xml`. As we saw before, the `dispatchEvent()` function queries the configuration object for available observers. Let's take a look at an example `config.xml` file:

```
<events>
    <event_name>
        <observers>
            <observer_identifier>
                <class>module_name/observer</class>
                <method>function_name</method>
            </observer_identifier>
        </observers>
    </event_name>
</events>
```

The `event` node can be specified in each of the configuration sections (admin, global, frontend, and so on) and we can specify multiple `event_name` children nodes; the `event_name` has to match the event name used in the `dispatchEvent()` function.

Inside each `event_name` node, we have a single observer node that can contain multiple observers, each with a unique identifier.

Observer nodes have two properties such as `<class>`, which points to our observer model class and `<method>`, which in turn points to the actual method inside the observer class. Let's analyze an example observer class definition:

```
class Namespace_Modulename_Model_Observer
{
    public function methodName(Varien_Event_Observer $observer)
    {
        //some code
    }
}
```

 One interesting thing about observer models is that they don't extend any other Magento class.

Summary

In this chapter, we covered many important and fundamental topics about Magento such as its architecture, folder structure, routing system, MVC patterns, events and observers, and configuration scopes.

And while this might seem overwhelming at first sight, it is just the tip of the iceberg. There is a lot more to learn about each of these topics and Magento. The purpose of this chapter is to make developers aware of all the important components of the platform from the configuration object up to the way the event/object pattern is implemented.

Magento is a powerful and flexible system, and it is much more than an e-commerce platform. The core team has put a lot of effort in making Magento a powerful framework.

In later chapters, we will not only review all these concepts in more detail, but we will also apply them in a practical manner by building our own extensions.

3
ORM and Data Collections

Collections and models are the bread and butter of everyday Magento development. In this chapter, we will introduce the reader to the Magento ORM system, and we will learn how to properly work with data collections and the EAV system. As with most modern systems, Magento implements an **Object Relational Mapping** (**ORM**) system.

> *Object-relational mapping (ORM, O/RM, and O/R mapping) in computer software is a programming technique for converting data between incompatible type systems in object-oriented programming languages. This creates, in effect, a "virtual object database" that can be used from within the programming language.*

In this chapter, we will cover the following topics:

- Magento Models
- Anatomy of a Magento Data Model
- EAV and EAV models
- Working with Direct SQL queries

We will also be working with several snippets of code to provide an easy framework to experiment and play around with Magento.

 Note that the interactive examples in this chapter assume you are working with either the default Magento installation inside the VagrantBox or a Magento installation with sample data.

For this purpose, I have created the **Interactive Magento Console (IMC)**, which is a shell script specially created for this book and inspired by Ruby's own **Interactive Ruby Console (IRB)**. Follow these steps:

1. The first thing we will need to do is to install the IMC. To do so, download the source files from `https://github.com/amacgregor/mdg_imc` and extract them under your Magento test installation. The IMC is a simple Magento shell script that will allow us to test our code in real time.

2. Once you extracted the script, log in to the shell of your virtualbox.

3. Next, we will need to navigate to our Magento root folder. If you are using the default vagrant box, the installation is already provided; the root folder is located under `/srv/www/ce1720/public_html/`, and we navigate to it by running the following command line:

   `$ cd /srv/www/ce1720/public_html`

4. Finally, we can start the IMC by running the following command line:

   `$ php shell/imc.php`

5. If everything is installed successfully, we should see a new line starting with `magento >`.

Magento Model Anatomy

As we learned in the previous chapter, Magento Data Models are used to manipulate and access the data. The model layer is divided into two fundamental types, simple models and EAV, where:

- **Simple Models**: These model implementations are simple mappings of one object to one table, meaning that our object attributes match each field and our table structure

- **Entity Attribute Value Models (EAV)**: These type of models are used to describe entities with a dynamic number of attributes

Note that it is important to clarify that not all Magento Models extend or Mage use the ORM. Observers are a clear example of simpler Model classes that are not mapped to a specific database table or entity.

In addition to that, each Model type is formed by the following layers:

- **Model class**: Here is where most of our business logic resides. Models are used to manipulate the data, but they don't access it directly.
- **Resource Model class**: Resource Models are used to interact with the database on behalf of our models. They are in charge of the actual CRUD operations.
- **Model Collection class**: Each Data Model has a collection class; collections are objects that hold a number of individual Magento Model instances.

 CRUD stands for the four basic types of database operations: create, read, update, and delete.

Magento Models don't contain any logic for communicating with the database; they are database agnostic. Instead, this code resides in the Resource Model layer.

This gives Magento the capacity to support different types of databases and platforms. Although currently only MySQL is officially supported, it is entirely possible to write a new resource class for a new database without touching any of the Model logic ones.

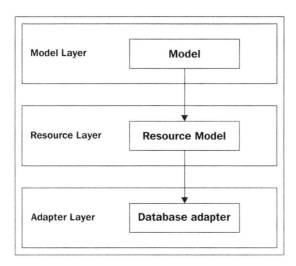

Let's experiment now by instantiating a product object and setting some of its properties by following these steps:

1. Start the Magento interactive console running under your Magento staging installation root:

```
php shell/imc.php
```

2. Our first step is going to create a new product object instance by typing:

```
magento> $product = Mage::getModel('catalog/product');
```

3. We can confirm whether this is a blank instance of the product class by running:

```
magento> echo get_class($product);
```

4. We should see the following as a successful output:

```
magento> Magento_Catalog_Model_Product
```

5. If we want to know more about the class methods, we can run the following command line:

```
magento> print_r(get_class_methods($product));
```

This will return an array with all the available methods inside the class. Let's try to run the following snippet of code and modify a product price and name:

```
$product = Mage::getModel('catalog/product')->load(2);
$name    = $product->getName() . '-TEST';
$price   = $product->getPrice();
$product->setPrice($price + 15);
$product->setName($name);
$product->save();
```

On the first line of code, we are instantiating a specific object, then we are proceeding to retrieve the name attribute from the object. Next, we are setting the price and name, and finally are saving the object.

If we open our Magento Product class Mage_Catalog_Model_Product, the first thing that we will notice is that while both getName() and getPrice() are defined inside our class, the setPrice() and setName() functions are not defined anywhere.

But why and more importantly, how is Magento magically defining each of the product object setter and getter methods? While getPrice() and getName() are indeed defined, there is no definition for any of the getter and setter methods for product attributes, such as color or manufacturer.

It's magic – methods

Well, it happens that the Magento ORM system is indeed using magic; or to be precise, one of the PHP's more powerful features for implementing its getters and setters, the magic `__call()` method. Magento methods that are used inside Magento are used to set, unset, check, or retrieve data.

When we try to call a method, which does not actually exist in our corresponding class, PHP will look into each of the parent classes for a declaration of that method. If we can't find the function on any of the parent classes, it will use its last resort and try to use a `__call()` method, and if found, Magento (or PHP for that matter) will call the magic method, thus passing the requested method name and its arguments.

Now, the Product model doesn't have a `__call()` method defined, but it gets one from the `Varien_Object` class from which all Magento models inherit from. The inheritance tree for the `Mage_Catalog_Model_Product` class is given in the following flowchart:

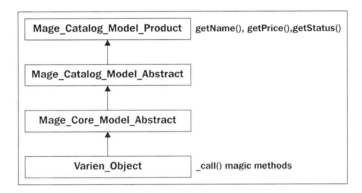

 Every Magento Model inherits from the `Varien_Object` class.

Let's take a closer look at the `Varien_Object` class:

1. Open the file located in `magento_root/lib/Varien/Object.php`.

2. The `Varien_Object` class not only has a `__call()` method but also two deprecated methods, `__set()` and `__get()`; these two are replaced by the `__call()` method and thus are no longer used.

```php
public function __call($method, $args)
{
    switch (substr($method, 0, 3)) {
        case 'get' :
```

```
        //Varien_Profiler::start('GETTER: '.get_
class($this).'::'.$method);
        $key = $this->_underscore(substr($method,3));
        $data = $this->getData($key, isset($args[0]) ? $args[0]
: null);
        //Varien_Profiler::stop('GETTER: '.get_
class($this).'::'.$method);
        return $data;

    case 'set' :
        //Varien_Profiler::start('SETTER: '.get_
class($this).'::'.$method);
        $key = $this->_underscore(substr($method,3));
        $result = $this->setData($key, isset($args[0]) ?
$args[0] : null);
        //Varien_Profiler::stop('SETTER: '.get_
class($this).'::'.$method);
        return $result;

    case 'uns' :
        //Varien_Profiler::start('UNS: '.get_
class($this).'::'.$method);
        $key = $this->_underscore(substr($method,3));
        $result = $this->unsetData($key);
        //Varien_Profiler::stop('UNS: '.get_
class($this).'::'.$method);
        return $result;
    case 'has' :
        //Varien_Profiler::start('HAS: '.get_
class($this).'::'.$method);
        $key = $this->_underscore(substr($method,3));
        //Varien_Profiler::stop('HAS: '.get_
class($this).'::'.$method);
        return isset($this->_data[$key]);
    }
    throw new Varien_Exception("Invalid method" . get_
class($this)."::".$method."(".print_r($args,1).")");
    }
```

Inside the __call() method, we have a switch that will handle not only getters and setters but also the unset and has functions.

If we start a debugger and follow the calls of our snippet code to the __call() method, we can see that it receives two arguments: the method name for example setName() and the arguments from the original call.

Interestingly, Magento tries to match the corresponding method type based on the first three letters of the method being called; this is done when the switch case argument calls the substring function:

```
substr($method, 0, 3)
```

The first thing that is called inside each case is the `_underscore()` function, which takes as parameter anything after the first three characters in the method name; following our example, the argument passed would be `Name`.

The `_underscore()` function returns a data key. This key is then used by each of the cases to manipulate the data. There are four basic data operations, each used on the corresponding switch case:

- `setData($parameters)`
- `getData($parameters)`
- `unsetData($parameters)`
- `isset($parameters)`

Each of these functions will interact with the `Varien_Object` data array and will manipulate it accordingly. In most cases, a magic set/get method will be used to interact with our object attributes; only in a few exceptions where additional business logic is required, getters and setters will be defined. In our example, they are `getName()` and `getPrice()`.

```
public function getPrice()
{
    if ($this->_calculatePrice || !$this >getData('price')) {
        return $this->getPriceModel()->getPrice($this);
    } else {
        return $this->getData('price');
    }
}
```

We will not enter details of what the price function is actually doing, but it clearly illustrates that additional logic might be required for certain parts of the models.

```
public function getName()
{
    return $this->_getData('name');
}
```

On the other hand, the getName() getter wasn't declared because of the need of implementing special logic but by the need of optimizing a crucial part of Magento. The Mage_Catalog_Model_Product getName() function can be potentially called hundreds of times per page load and is one of the most commonly used functions across Magento; after all, what kind of e-commerce platform would it be if it was not centered around products?

Frontend and backend alike will call the getName() function at one point or another. For example, if we load a category page with 24 products, that is, 24 separate calls to the getName() function, each of these calls will look for a getName() method on each of the parent classes, and then, when we try to use magic __call() method, it will result in losing precious milliseconds.

Resource Models contain all the database-specific logic, and they instantiate the specific read and write adapters for their corresponding data source. Let's go back to our example working with products and take a look at the product Resource Model located at Mage_Catalog_Model_Resource_Product.

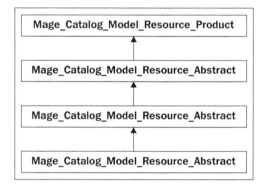

Resource models come in two different types: Entity and MySQL4. The latter being a pretty standard one-table/one-model association, while the former is far more complicated.

EAV Model

EAV stands for entity, attribute, and value, it is probably the most difficult concept for new Magento developers to grasp. While the EAV concept is not unique to Magento, it is rarely implemented on modern systems, on top of that, Magento implementation is not a simple one.

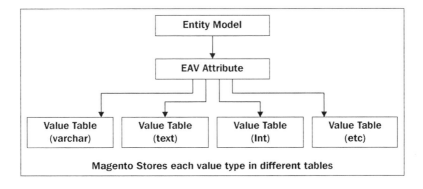

Magento Stores each value type in different tables

What is EAV?

In order to understand what EAV is and what its role within Magento is, we need to break down it into the parts of the EAV model.

- **Entity**: The entity represents the data items (objects) inside Magento products, customers, categories, and orders. Each entity is stored in the database with a unique ID.

- **Attribute**: These are our object properties. Instead of having one column per attribute on the product table, attributes are stored on separates sets of tables.

- **Value**: As the name implies, it is simply the value link to a particular attribute.

This design pattern is the secret behind Magento's flexibility and power, allowing entities to add and remove new properties without having to do any changes to the code or templates.

Whereas model can be seen as a vertical way of growing our database (new attributes add more rows), the traditional model would involve a horizontal grow pattern (new attributes add more columns) that would result in a schema redesign every time new attributes are added.

The EAV model not only allows the fast evolution of our database, but also, it is more efficient, because it only works with non-empty attributes, avoiding the need to reserve additional space in the database for null values.

 If you are interested in exploring and learning more about the Magento database structure, I highly recommend you to visit www.magereverse.com.

Adding a new product attribute is as simple as going to the Magento backend and specifying the new attribute type, be it color, size, brand, and so on. The opposite is also true, because we can get rid of unused attributes on our products or customer models.

 For more information on managing attributes, visit http://www. magentocommerce.com/knowledge-base/entry/how-do-attributes-work-in-magento.

Magento Community Edition currently has eight different types of EAV objects:

- Customer
- Customer address
- Products
- Product categories
- Orders
- Invoices
- Credit memos
- Shipments

 Magento Enterprise Edition has one additional type called RMA item, which is part of the **Return Merchandise Authorization (RMA)** system.

All this flexibility and power is not free, and there is a price to pay; implementing the EAV model results in having our entity data distributed on a large number of tables, for example, just the Product Model is distributed on around 40 different tables.

The following diagram only shows a few of the tables involved in saving the information of Magento products:

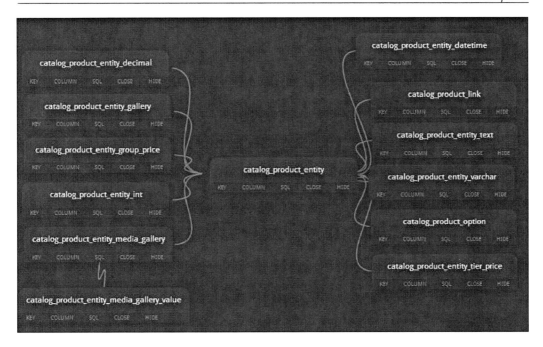

Another major downside of EAV is the loss of performance when retrieving large collections of EAV objects and an increase on the database query complexity. Since the data is more fragmented (stored in more tables), selecting a single record involves several joins.

Let's continue using Magento products as our example and manually build the query for retrieving a single product.

If you have PHPMyAdmin or MySQL Workbench installed on your development environment, you can experiment with the following queries. Each can be downloaded from PHPMyAdmin (`http://www.phpmyadmin.net/`) and MySQL Workbench (`http://www.mysql.com/products/workbench/`).

The first table that we will need to use is the `catalog_product_entity`. We can consider this as our main product EAV table since it contains the main entity records for our products:

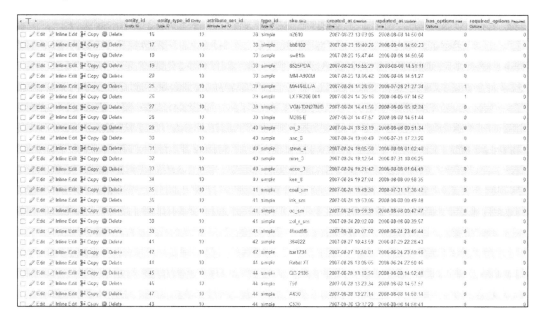

Let's query the table by running the following SQL query:

```
SELECT * FROM `catalog_product_entity`;
```

The table contains the following fields:

- `entity_id`: This is our product unique identifier and is used internally by Magento.

- `entity_type_id`: Magento has several different types of EAV models, products, customers, and orders, and these are just some of them. Identifying each by type allows Magento to retrieve the attributes and values from the appropriate tables.

- `attribute_set_id`: Products attributes can be grouped locally into attribute sets. Attribute sets allow even further flexibility on the product structure since products are not forced to use all available attributes.

- `type_id`: There are several different types of products in Magento: simple, configurable, bundled, downloadable, and grouped products, each with unique settings and functionality.

- `sku`: **Stock Keeping Unit (SKU)** is a number or code used to identify each unique product or item for sale in a store. This is a user-defined value.

- `has_options`: This is used to identify if a product has custom options.

- `required_options`: This is used to identify if any of the custom options are required.

- `created_at`: This is a row creation date.

- `updated_at`: This shows the last time the row was modified.

Now we have a basic understanding of the product entity table, and we also know that each record represents a single product in our Magento store, but we don't have much information about that product beyond the SKU and the product type.

So, where are the attributes stored? And how does Magento know the difference between a product attribute and a customer attribute?

For that, we need to take a look at the `eav_attribute` table by running the following SQL query:

```
SELECT * FROM `eav_attribute`;
```

As a result, we will not only see the product attributes but also attributes corresponding to the customer model, order model, and so on. Fortunately, we already have a key for filtering the attributes from this table. Let's run the following query:

```
SELECT * FROM `eav_attribute`
WHERE entity_type_id = 4;
```

This query is telling the database to only retrieve the attributes where the `entity_type_id` columns are equal to the product `entity_type_id(4)`. Before moving on, let's analyze the most important fields inside the `eav_attribute` table:

- `attribute_id`: This is the unique identifier for each attribute and primary key of the table.

- `entity_type_id`: This field relates each attribute to a specific EAV model type.

- `attribute_code`: This field is the name or key of our attribute and is used to generate the getters and setters for our magic methods.

- `backend_model`: The backend model manages loading and storing data into the database.

- `backend_type`: This field specifies the type of value stored into the backend (database).

- `backend_table`: This field is used to specify if the attribute should be stored on a special table instead of the default EAV tables.

- `frontend_model`: The frontend model handles the rendering of the attribute element into a web browser.

- `frontend_input`: Similar to the frontend model, the frontend input specifies the type of input field the web browser should render.

- `frontend_label`: This field is the label/name of the attribute as it should be rendered by the browser.

- `source_model`: The source models are used to populate an attribute with possible values. Magento comes with several predefined source models for countries, yes or no values, regions, and so on.

Retrieving the data

At this point, we have successfully retrieved a product entity and the specific attributes that apply to that entity, and now it is time to start retrieving the actual values. In order to simply execute the example (and the query), we will only try to retrieve the name attribute of our products.

But how do we know on which table our attribute values are stored? Well, thankfully, Magento is following a naming convention for naming the tables. If we inspect our database structure, we will notice that there are several tables using the `catalog_product_entity` prefix:

- `catalog_product_entity`
- `catalog_product_entity_datetime`
- `catalog_product_entity_decimal`
- `catalog_product_entity_int`
- `catalog_product_entity_text`
- `catalog_product_entity_varchar`
- `catalog_product_entity_gallery`
- `catalog_product_entity_media_gallery`
- `catalog_product_entity_tier_price`

But, wait, how do we know which is the right table to query for our name attribute values? If you were paying attention, we've already seen the answer. Do you remember that the `eav_attribute` table had a column called `backend_type`?

Magento EAV stores each attribute on a different table based on the backend type of that attribute. If we want to confirm the backend type of our name, we can do so by running the following code:

```
SELECT * FROM `eav_attribute`
WHERE `entity_type_id` =4 AND `attribute_code` = 'name';
```

And we should see, as a result, that the backend type is varchar and that the values for this attribute are stored in the catalog_product_entity_varchar table. Let's inspect this table:

	value_id Value ID	entity_type_id Entity Type ID	attribute_id Attribute ID	store_id Store ID	entity_id Entity ID	value Value
Edit Inline Edit Copy Delete	1	3	35	0	1	Root Catalog
Edit Inline Edit Copy Delete	2	3	35	1	1	Root Catalog
Edit Inline Edit Copy Delete	3	3	37	1	1	root-catalog
Edit Inline Edit Copy Delete	4	3	35	0	2	Default Category
Edit Inline Edit Copy Delete	5	3	35	1	2	Default Category
Edit Inline Edit Copy Delete	6	3	43	1	2	PRODUCTS
Edit Inline Edit Copy Delete	7	3	37	1	2	default-category
Edit Inline Edit Copy Delete	8	3	35	0	3	Clothing
Edit Inline Edit Copy Delete	9	3	37	0	3	clothing
Edit Inline Edit Copy Delete	10	3	40	0	3	NULL
Edit Inline Edit Copy Delete	11	3	43	0	3	PRODUCTS
Edit Inline Edit Copy Delete	12	3	60	0	3	position
Edit Inline Edit Copy Delete	13	3	52	0	3	NULL
Edit Inline Edit Copy Delete	14	3	55	0	3	two_columns_left
Edit Inline Edit Copy Delete	15	3	35	0	4	Tops
Edit Inline Edit Copy Delete	16	3	37	0	4	tops
Edit Inline Edit Copy Delete	17	3	40	0	4	NULL
Edit Inline Edit Copy Delete	18	3	43	0	4	PRODUCTS
Edit Inline Edit Copy Delete	19	3	52	0	4	NULL
Edit Inline Edit Copy Delete	20	3	55	0	4	NULL
Edit Inline Edit Copy Delete	21	3	35	0	5	Bottoms
Edit Inline Edit Copy Delete	22	3	37	0	5	bottoms
Edit Inline Edit Copy Delete	23	3	40	0	5	NULL
Edit Inline Edit Copy Delete	24	3	43	0	5	PRODUCTS
Edit Inline Edit Copy Delete	25	3	52	0	5	NULL
Edit Inline Edit Copy Delete	26	3	55	0	5	NULL
Edit Inline Edit Copy Delete	27	3	35	0	6	Intimates
Edit Inline Edit Copy Delete	28	3	37	0	6	intimates
Edit Inline Edit Copy Delete	29	3	40	0	6	NULL
Edit Inline Edit Copy Delete	30	3	43	0	6	PRODUCTS

The catalog_product_entity_varchar table is formed by only six columns:

- value_id: The attribute value is the unique identifier and a primary key
- entity_type_id: This value belongs to the entity type ID
- attribute_id: This is a foreign key that relates the value with our eav_entity table

- `store_id`: This is a foreign key matching an attribute value with a storeview

- `entity_id`: This is a foreign key to the corresponding entity table; in this case, it is `catalog_product_entity`

- `value`: This is the actual value that we want to retrieve

 Depending on the attribute configuration, we can have it as a global value, meaning it applies across all store views or a value per storeview.

Now that we finally have all the tables that we need to retrieve the product information, we can build our query:

```
SELECT p.entity_id AS product_id, var.value AS product_name, p.sku AS
product_sku
FROM catalog_product_entity p, eav_attribute eav, catalog_product_
entity_varchar var
WHERE p.entity_type_id = eav.entity_type_id
    AND var.entity_id = p.entity_id
    AND eav.attribute_code = 'name'
    AND eav.attribute_id = var.attribute_id
```

product_id	product_name	product_sku
16	Nokia 2610 Phone	n2610
17	BlackBerry 8100 Pearl	bb8100
18	Sony Ericsson W810i	sw810i
19	AT&T 8525 PDA	8525PDA
20	Samsung MM-A900M Ace	MM-A900M
25	Apple MacBook Pro MA464LL/A 15.4" Notebook PC	MA464LL/A
26	Acer Ferrari 3200 Notebook Computer PC	LX.FR206.001
27	Sony VAIO VGN-TXN27N/B 11.1" Notebook PC	VGN-TXN27N/B
28	Toshiba M285-E 14"	M285-E
29	CN Clogs Beach/Garden Clog	cn_3
30	ASICS® Men's GEL-Kayano® XII	asc_8
31	Steven by Steve Madden Pryme Pump	steve_4
32	Nine West Women's Lucero Pump	nine_3
33	ECCO Womens Golf Flexor Golf Shoe	ecco_3
34	Kenneth Cole New York Men's Con-verge Slip-on	ken_8
35	Coalesce: Functioning On Impatience T-Shirt	coal_sm
36	Ink Eater: Krylon Bombear Destroyed Tee	ink_sm
37	The Only Children: Paisley T-Shirt	oc_sm
38	Zolof The Rock And Roll Destroyer: LOL Cat T-shirt	zol_r_sm
39	The Get Up Kids: Band Camp Pullover Hoodie	4fasd5f5
41	Akio Dresser	384822
42	Barcelona Bamboo Platform Bed	bar1234

As result of our query, we should see a result set with three columns: `product_id`, `product_name`, and `product_sku`. So, let's step back for a second in order to get product names with SKUs. With raw SQL, we would have to write a five-line SQL query, and we would only be retrieving two values from our products: from one single EAV value table if we wanted to retrieve a numeric field, such as price, or from a text value, such as product.

If we didn't have an ORM in place, maintaining Magento would be almost impossible. Fortunately, we do have an ORM in place, and most likely, you will never need to deal with raw SQL for working with Magento.

That said, let's see how can we retrieve the same product information by using the Magento ORM:

1. Our first step is going to instantiate a product collection:

   ```
   $collection = Mage::getModel('catalog/product')->getCollection();
   ```

2. Then, we will specifically tell Magento to select the name attribute:

   ```
   $collection->addAttributeToSelect('name');
   ```

3. Now sort the collection by name:

   ```
   $collection->setOrder('name', 'asc');
   ```

4. And, finally, we will tell Magento to load the collection:

   ```
   $collection->load();
   ```

5. The end result is a collection of all products in the store sorted by name; we can inspect the actual SQL query by running:

   ```
   echo $collection->getSelect()->__toString();
   ```

With the help of only three lines of code, we are able to tell Magento to grab all the products in the store to specifically select the name, and finally, order the products by the name.

> The last line, `$collection->getSelect()->__toString()`, allows us to see the actual query that Magento is executing on our behalf.

The actual query being generated by Magento is:

```
SELECT `e`.*. IF( at_name.value_id >0, at_name.value, at_name_default.
value ) AS `name`
FROM `catalog_product_entity` AS `e`
LEFT JOIN `catalog_product_entity_varchar` AS `at_name_default` ON
(`at_name_default`.`entity_id` = `e`.`entity_id`)
```

```
AND (`at_name_default`.`attribute_id` = '65')
AND `at_name_default`.`store_id` =0
LEFT JOIN `catalog_product_entity_varchar` AS `at_name` ON ( `at_
name`.`entity_id` = `e`.`entity_id` )
AND (`at_name`.`attribute_id` = '65')
AND (`at_name`.`store_id` =1)
ORDER BY `name` ASC
```

As we can see, the ORM and the EAV models are wonderful tools that not only put a lot of power and flexibility on hands of the developers, but they also do it in a way that is comprehensive and easy to use.

Working with Magento collections

If you look back to the previous code example, you might notice that we've not only instantiated a Product model, but also we've called the getCollection() method. The getCollection() method is part of the Mage_Core_Model_Abstract class, meaning that every single model inside Magento can call this method.

 All collections inherit from Varien_Data_Collection.

A Magento collection is basically a model that contains other models. So, instead of using an array for holding a collection of products, we could use a Product collection instead. Collections not only provide a convenient data structure for grouping models but also provide special methods that we can use to manipulate and work with collection of entities.

Some of the most useful collection methods are:

- addAttributeToSelect: To add an attribute to entities in a collection, * can be used as a wildcard to add all available attributes

- addFieldToFilter: To add an attribute filter to a collection, this function is used on regular, non-EAV models

- addAttributeToFilter: This method is used to filter a collection of EAV entities

- addAttributeToSort: This method is used to add an attribute to sort order

- `addStoreFilter`: This method is used to store an availability filter; it includes the availability product
- `addWebsiteFilter`: This method is used to add a website filter to a collection
- `addCategoryFilter`: This method is used to specify a category filter for a product collection
- `addUrlRewrite`: This method is used to add URL rewrites data to a product
- `setOrder`: This method is used to set the sorting order of a collection

Those are just a few of the collection methods available; each collection implements different unique methods depending on the entity type they correspond to. For example, the customer collection `Mage_Customer_Model_Resource_Customer_Collection` has a unique method called `groupByEmail()`, which has the name that correctly implies and groups the entities inside of a collection by e-mail.

As with previous examples, we will continue working with the product models, and in this case, the product collection.

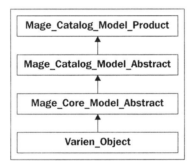

In order to illustrate better how we can use collection, we will be working on the following common product scenarios:

1. Get product collection only from a specific category.
2. Get new products since X date.
3. Get Bestseller products.
4. Filter product collection by visibility.
5. Filter products without image.
6. Add multiple sort orders.

Get product collection only from a specific category

The first thing most developers try to do when starting with Magento is to load a product collection with products from only a specific category, and while I have seen many approaches by using addCategoryFilter() or addAttributeToFilter(), the reality is that, for most cases, the approach is much simpler and a bit counter-intuitive to what we have learned so far.

The easiest way of doing it is not by getting a product collection first and then filtering by a category but actually instantiating our target category and getting the product collection from there. Let's run the following snippet of code on IMC:

```
$category = Mage::getModel('catalog/category')->load(5);
$productCollection = $category->getProductCollection();
```

We can find the getProductCollection() method declaration inside the Mage_Catalog_Model_Category class. Let's take a better look at this method:

```
public function getProductCollection()
{
    $collection = Mage::getResourceModel('catalog/product_collection')
        ->setStoreId($this->getStoreId())
        ->addCategoryFilter($this);
    return $collection;
}
```

As we can see, the function does nothing more than instantiating a Resource Model for the product collection, that is, setting the store to the current store ID and passing the current category to the addCategoryFilter() method.

This is one of those decisions that was taken to optimize Magento performance, and frankly to simplify the life of the developers working with it, since in most cases a category is going to be available one way or the other.

Get new products added since X date

So, now that we know how to get a product collection from a specific category, let's see whether we are able to apply filters to the resulting products and only to the retrieved ones matching our conditions; in this particular case, we will request all the products that were added after December 2012. Following our previous example code, we can filter our collection by product creation date by running the following code on IMC:

```
// Product collection from our previous example
$productCollection->addFieldToFilter('created_at', array('from' =>
'2012-12-01'));
```

It is simple, isn't it? We could even add an additional condition and get the products added between two dates. Let's say we only want to retrieve the products that were created in the month of December:

```
$productCollection->addFieldToFilter('created_at', array('from' =>
'2012-12-01));
$productCollection->addFieldToFilter('created_at', array('to' =>
'2012-12-30'));
```

Magento's `addFieldToFilter` supports the following conditions:

Attribute code	SQL condition
eq	=
neq	!=
like	LIKE
nlike	NOT LIKE
in	IN ()
nin	NOT IN ()
is	IS
notnull	NOT NULL
null	NULL
moreq	>=
gt	>
lt	<
gteq	>=
lteq	<=

We can try other types of filters, for example, let's use the following code on IMC after adding our creating date filter, so we can retrieve only visible products:

```
$productCollection->addAttributeToFilter('visibility', 4);
```

The visibility attribute is a special attribute used by products to control where products are shown; it has the following values:

- **Not visible individually**: It has a value 1
- **Catalog**: It has a value 2
- **Search**: It has a value 3
- **Catalog and Search**: It has a value 4

Get Bestseller products

To try to get the Bestseller products for a specific category, we would need to step up our game and do a join with the `sales_order` table. Retrieving Bestseller products will come in handy later on for creating a special category or custom reporting; we can run the following code on IMC:

```
$category = Mage::getModel('catalog/category')->load(5);
$productCollection = $category->getProductCollection();
$productCollection->getSelect()
            ->join(array('o'=> 'sales_flat_order_item'), 'main_table.
entity_id = o.product_id', array('o.row_total','o.product_id'))-
>group(array('sku'));
```

Let's analyze what's happening on the third line of our snippet. `getSelect()` is a method inherited directly from `Varien_Data_Collection_Db`, which returns the variable where the `Select` statement is stored in addition to the collections that provide methods for specifying a join and a group without having to write any SQL.

This is not the only way of adding a join to a collection. There is, in fact, a cleaner way of doing it by using the `joinField()` function. Let's rewrite our previous code to make use of this function:

```
$category = Mage::getModel('catalog/category')->load(5);
$productCollection = $category->getProductCollection();
$productCollection->joinField('o', 'sales_flat_order_item', array('o.
row_total','o.product_id'), 'main_table.entity_id = o.product_id')
->group(array('sku'));
```

Filter product collection by visibility

This is extremely easy to do with the help of the `addAttributeToFilter`. Magento products have a system attribute called visibility, which has four possible number values ranging from 1 to 4. We are interested only in showing products whose visibility is 4; meaning, it can be seen both in the search results and the catalog. Let's run the following code in IMC:

```
$category = Mage::getModel('catalog/category')->load(5);
$productCollection = $category->getProductCollection();
$productCollection->addAttributeToFilter('visibility', 4);
```

If we change the visibility code, we can compare the different collections results.

Filter products without images

Filtering products without images comes in handy when you are dealing with a third-party import system, which can sometimes be unreliable. As with everything we have done so far, product images are the attributes of our product.

```
$category = Mage::getModel('catalog/category')->load(5);
$productCollection = $category->getProductCollection();
$productCollection->addAttributeToFilter('small_image',array('notnull'
=>'','neq'=>'no_selection'));
```

By adding that extra filter, we require products to have a small image specified; by default, Magento has three products: image types, thumbnail, and `small_image` and image. These three types are used on different parts of the application. We could even set up a stricter rule for products if we wanted to.

```
$productCollection->addAttributeToFilter('small_image',
array('notnull'=>'','neq'=>'no_selection'));
->addAttributeToFilter('thumbnail, array('notnull'=>'','neq'=>'no_
selection'))
->addAttributeToFilter('image', array('notnull'=>'','neq'=>'no_
selection'));
```

Only products that have all the three types of images will be included in our collection. Try experimenting by filtering with the different image types.

Add multiple sort orders

Finally, let's take our collection and sort it first by stock status and then by price, from highest to lowest. In order to retrieve the stock status information, we will use a method unique to the stock status resource model called `addStockStatusToSelect()`, which will take care of generating the corresponding SQL for our collection query:

```
$category = Mage::getModel('catalog/category')->load(5);
$productCollection = $category->getProductCollection();
$select = $productCollection->getSelect();
Mage::getResourceModel('cataloginventory/stock_status')->addStockStatu
sToSelect($select, Mage::app()->getWebsite());
$select->order('salable desc');
$select->order('price asc');
```

Inside this query, Magento will sort products by the salable status that is either true or false, and by price; the end result is that all the available products will show the first ordered ones from the most expensive to the cheapest ones, and then, the out-of-stock products will be shown from the most expensive to the cheapest.

Experiment with different sort order combinations to see how Magento organizes and orders the product collections.

Using Direct SQL

So far, we have learned how Magento data models and the ORM system provide a clean and simple way to access, store, and manipulate our data. Before we jump right into this section, learn about the Magento database adapters, and how to run raw SQL queries, I feel it is important that we understand why you should avoid as much as possible to use what you are about to learn in this section.

Magento is an extremely complex system, and as we've also learned in the previous chapter, a framework is driven in part by events; just saving a product will trigger different events, each doing a different task. This will not happen if you decide to just create a query and update a product directly. So, as developers, we have to be extremely careful and sure whether there is a justifiable reason for going outside the ORM.

That said, there are, of course, scenarios when being able to work with the database directly comes in extremely handy and is actually simpler than working with the Magento models. For example, when updating a product attribute globally or changing a product collection status, we could load a product collection and loop through each of the individual products updating and saving them. While this would work fine on a smaller collection, as soon we start growing and working with a larger dataset, our performance would start to drop and the script would take several seconds to execute.

On the other hand, a direct SQL query will execute much faster, usually under 1 second, depending on the dataset size and the query being executed.

Out of the box, Magento will take care of all the heavy lifting of having to establish a connection to the database by using the `Mage_Core_Model_Resource` model; Magento makes two types of connections available to us, `core_read` and `core_write`.

Let's start by instantiating a resource model and two connections, one for reading and the other for writing:

```
$resource = Mage::getModel('core/resource');
$read = $resource->getConnection('core_read');
$write = $resource->getConnection('core_write');
```

Even if we are working with direct SQL queries, thanks to Magento, we don't have to worry about setting up the connection to the DB beyond instantiating a resource model and the proper type of connection.

Reading

Let's test our read connection by executing the following code:

```
$resource = Mage::getModel('core/resource');
$read = $resource->getConnection('core_read');
$query = 'SELECT * FROM catalog_product_entity';
$results = $read->fetchAll($query);
```

Although this query works, it will return all the products in the `catalog_product_entity` table. But what will happen if we try to run this same code on a Magento installation that uses table prefixes? Or what if Magento suddenly changes the table name in the next upgrade? This code is not portable or easily maintainable. Fortunately, the resource model provides another handy method called `getTableName()`.

`getTableName()` method will take a factory name as a parameter, and based on the configuration established by the `config.xml`, it will not only find out the right table but will also verify that table exists in the DB. Let's update our code to use `getTableName()`:

```
$resource = Mage::getModel('core/resource');
$read = $resource->getConnection('core_read');
$query = 'SELECT * FROM ' . $resource->getTableName('catalog/
product');
$results = $read->fetchAll($query);
```

We are also using the `fetchAll()` method. This will return all the rows of our query as an array, but this is not the only option available; we also have `fetchCol()` and `fetchOne()` at our disposal. Let's have a look at the following functions:

- `fetchAll`: This function retrieves all the rows returned by the original query
- `fetchOne`: This function will return only the values from the first database row returned by the query
- `fetchCol`: This function will return all the rows returned by the query but only the first rows; this is useful if you only want to retrieve a single column with unique identifiers such as products IDs or SKUs

Writing

As we've mentioned before, saving a model, be it a product, category, customer, and so on, in Magento can be relatively slow due to the amount of observers and events triggered in the backend.

But if we are only looking to update simple static values, updating large collections can be a painfully slow process if done through the Magento ORM. Let's say, for example, we want to make all the products on the site out of stock. Instead of doing it through the Magento backend or creating a custom script that iterates through a collection of all the products, we can simply perform the following code snippet:

```
$resource = Mage::getModel('core/resource');
$read = $resource->getConnection('core_write);
$tablename = $resource->getTableName('cataloginventory/stock_status');
$query = 'UPDATE {$tablename} SET `is_in_stock` = 1';
$write->query($query);
```

Summary

In this chapter, we have learned about:

- Magento Models, their inheritance, and purpose
- How Magento uses resource and collection models
- The EAV model and its importance within Magento
- How the EAV works and the structure that is used inside the database
- What the Magento ORM model is and how it is implemented
- How to work with Direct SQL and the Magento resource adapter

The chapters so far have been more theoretic than practical; this has been done with the intention of guiding you through the complexity of Magento and providing you with the tools and knowledge that you will require for the rest of the book. For the rest of the book, we will take a more hands-on approach and start building extensions incrementally, applying all the concepts we have learned so far.

In the next chapter, we will start getting our feet wet and develop our first Magento extension.

4
Frontend Development

So far, we have focused on the theory behind Magento, its architecture, and getting familiar with common and important concepts of everyday Magento development.

In this chapter, we will give a practical use to the skills and knowledge we have acquired so far by incrementally building a Magento extension for our frontend. We will build a fully functional Gift Registry extension.

Extending Magento

Before jumping ahead and start building our extension, let's define an example scenario and a scope for our extension. This way we will have a clear idea of what we are building and more importantly, of what we are not building.

Scenario

Our scenario is simple; we want to extend Magento to allow customers to create gift registry lists and share them with friends and family. Customers should be able to create multiple gift registries and specify the recipients of those gift registries.

A gift registry will hold the following information:

- Event type
- Event name
- Event date
- Event location
- List of products

Features

Have a look at the following features:

- Store administrator can define multiple event types (birthdays, weddings, and gift registries)
- Create events and assign multiple gift registry lists to each event
- Customers can add products to their registries from the cart, wish list, or directly from the product pages
- Customers can have multiple gift registries
- People can share their registries with friends and family through e-mail and/or direct link
- Friends and family can buy the items from the gift registry

Further improvements

The following is a list of possible features that have been left out of this example extension due to their complexity, or in the case of social media due to the fact that their APIs and the amount of social media platforms is ever-changing, but they are still a good challenge for readers who want to extend this module even further:

- Social media integration
- The registry can keep track of the request and fulfilled quantities for each registry item
- Specify multiple and different registry owners
- Delivery to registry owner address

Hello Magento

In previous chapters, we learned about the Magento code pools (core, community, local). Since we don't intend to distribute our module on Magento Connect, we will be creating it under the local directory.

All Magento modules are kept inside packages or namespaces; for example, all the Core Magento modules are kept under the Mage namespace. For the purpose of this book, we will use **Magento Developers Guide (MDG)**.

The Magento naming convention for modules is `Namespace_Modulename`.

Our next step will be to create the module structure and configuration files. We need to create a namespace directory under `app/code/local/`. The namespace can be anything you like. The accepted convention is to use the company's name or the author's name as the namespace. So our first step will be to create the directory `app/code/local/Mdg/`. This directory will also hold not only our gift registry module but also any future modules we develop.

Under our namespace directory, we will also need to create a new directory with the name of our module, which will hold all the code of custom extension.

So let's go ahead and create a `Giftregistry` directory. Once that is done, let's create the rest of our directory structure.

 Note that Magento is a bit sensitive to the use of camel-casing due to its use of factory methods. In general, it's a good idea to avoid using camel—casing in our module/controller/action names. For more information on Magento naming conventions, please see the *Appendix* of this book.

The file location is `/app/code/local/Mdg/Giftregistry/`.

```
Block/
Controller/
controllers/
Helper/
etc/
Model/
sql/
```

As we have learned so far, Magento uses `.xml` files as a central part of its configuration. In order for a module to be recognized and activated by Magento, we need to create a single file under `app/etc/modules/`, following the `Namespace_Modulename.xml` convention. Let's create our file.

The file location is `app/etc/modules/Mdg_Giftregistry.xml`.

```xml
<?xml version="1.0"?>
<config>
    <modules>
        <Mdg_Giftregistry>
            <active>true</active>
            <codePool>local</codePool>
        </Mdg_Giftregistry >
    </modules>
</config>
```

Downloading the example code

You can download the example code files for all Packt books you have purchased from your account at `http://www.packtpub.com`. If you purchased this book elsewhere, you can visit `http://www.packtpub.com/support` and register to have the files e-mailed directly to you.

After creating this file or making any changes to our module configuration files, we will need to refresh the Magento configuration cache:

1. Navigate to the Magento backend.
2. Open **System | Cache Management**.
3. Click on **Flush Magento**.

Since we are working on a development extension and we are going to be making frequent changes to the configuration and extension code, it is a good idea to disable the cache. Follow these steps:

1. Navigate to the Magento Backend.
2. Open **System | Cache Management**.
3. Select all the **Cache Type** checkboxes.
4. Select **Disable** from the **Actions** drop-down list.
5. Click on the **Submit** button.

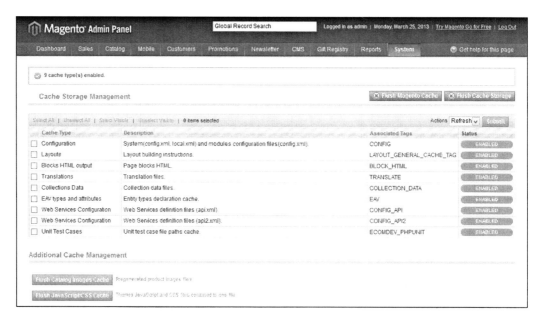

Once we have cleared the cache, we can confirm that our extension is being made active by going into **System | Advanced**.

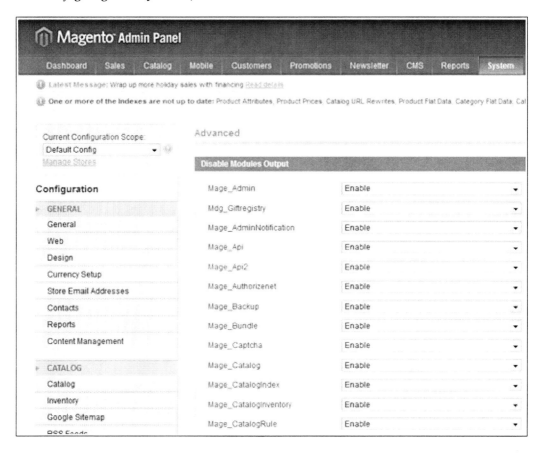

Magento now knows about our module, but we haven't told Magento what our module is supposed to do; for that, we will need to set up the module configuration.

XML module configuration

There are two main files involved in a module configuration: `config.xml` and `system.xml`. In addition to these module configurations, these are also stored in:

- `api.xml`
- `adminhtml.xml`
- `cache.xml`
- `widget.xml`
- `wsdl.xml`
- `wsi.xml`
- `convert.xml`

In this chapter, we will focus only on the `config.xml` file. Let's create our base file and break down each of the nodes by following these steps:

1. Start by creating the `config.xml` file under our module `etc/directory`.

2. Now, copy the following code to the `config.xml` file (the file location is `app/code/local/Mdg/Giftregistry/etc/config.xml`):

```xml
<?xml version="1.0"?>
<config>
    <modules>
        <Mdg_Giftregistry>
            <version>0.1.0</version>
        </Mdg_Giftregistry>
    </modules>
    <global>
        <models>
            <mdg_giftregistry>
                <class>Mdg_Giftregistry_Model</class>
            </mdg_giftregistry>
        </models>
        <blocks>
            <mdg_giftregistry>
                <class>Mdg_Giftregistry_Block</class>
            </mdg_giftregistry>
        </blocks>
        <helpers>
            <mdg_giftregistry>
                <class>Mdg_Giftregistry_Helper</class>
            </mdg_giftregistry>
        </helpers>
```

```
        <resources>
            <mdg_giftregistry_setup>
                <setup>
                    <module>Mdg_Giftregistry</module>
                </setup>
            </mdg_giftregistry_setup>
        </resources>
    </global>
</config>
```

All module configurations are contained inside the `<config>` node. Inside this node, we have the `<global>` and `<modules>` nodes.

The `<modules>` node is just used to specify the current module version, which is later used to decide which installation and upgrade files to run.

There are three main configuration nodes that are most commonly used to specify the configuration scope:

*   `<global>`
*   `<adminhtml>`
*   `<frontend>`

For now, we will be working on the `<global>` scope. This will make any configuration available to both, the Magento Frontend and Backend. Under the `<global>` node, we have the following nodes:

*   `<models>`
*   `<blocks>`
*   `<helpers>`
*   `<resources>`

As we can see, each node follows the same configuration pattern:

```
<context>
    <factory_alias>
        <class>NameSpace_ModuleName_ClassType</class>
    </factory_alias>
</context>
```

Each of the nodes that are used by the Magento class factories instantiate our custom objects. The `<factory_alias>` node is a critical part of our extension configuration. The `<factory_alias>` node is used by the factory methods, such as `Mage::getModel()` or `Mage::getHelper()`.

Notice that we are not defining each specific Model, Block, or Helper, just the path where Magento factories can find them. Magento naming convention allows us to have any folder structure under each of these folders, and Magento will be smart enough to load the appropriate class in Magento's class names.

 In Magento, class names and directory structures are one and the same.

For example, we could have created a new model class under `app/code/local/Mdg/Giftregistry/Models/Folder1/Folder2/Folder3`, and the factory name for instantiating an object from this class would be:

```
Mage::getModel('mdg_giftregistry/folder1_folder2_folder3_classname');
```

Let's create our first model, or to be more specific, a helper class. Helpers are used to contain utility methods that are used to perform common tasks and can be shared among different classes.

Let's go ahead and create an empty `helper` class; we will add the helper logic later in this chapter.

The file location is `app/code/loca/Mdg/Giftregistry/Helper/Data.php`. Refer to the following code:

```php
<?php
class Mdg_Giftregistry_Helper_Data extends Mage_Core_Helper_Abstract {

}
?>
```

It might seem odd that we are naming our helper `Data`, but this is actually part of Magento's standards that each module has a default `helper` class called `Data`. Another interesting thing with `helper` classes is that we can just pass the `<factory_alias>` node without a class-specific class name to the `helper` factory method, and this will default to the `Data` helper class.

So if we wanted to instantiate our default `helper` class, we only need to perform the following:

```
Mage::helper('mdg_registry');
```

Models and saving data

Before jumping straight into creating our models, we need to define clearly what type of models we are going to build and how many. So let's review our example scenario. For our gift registry, it appears that we will need two different models:

- **Registry Model**: This model is used to store the gift registry information, such as gift registry type, address, and recipient information
- **Registry Item**: This model is used to store the information of each of the gift registry items (quantity requested, quantity bought, `product_id`)

Although this approach is correct, it does not meet all the requirements of our example scenario. By having all the registry information stored into a single table, we cannot add more registry types without modifying the code.

So, in this case, we will want to break down our data into multiple tables:

- **Registry Entity**: This table is used to store the gift registry and event information
- **Registry Type**: By storing the gift registry type into a separate table, we can add or remove event types
- **Registry Item**: This table is used to store the information of each of the gift registry items (quantity requested, quantity bought, `product_id`)

Now that we have defined our data structure, we can start building the corresponding models that will allow us to access and manipulate our data.

Creating the models

Let's start by creating the Gift Registry type model, which is used to manage the registry types (wedding, birthday, baby shower, and so on). To do so, follow these steps:

1. Navigate to the `Model` folder on our module directory.
2. Create a new file called `Type.php` and copy the following content into the file (the file location is `app/code/local/Mdg/Giftregistry/Model/Type.php`):

```php
<?php
class Mdg_Giftregistry_Model_Type extends Mage_Core_Model_Abstract
{
    public function __construct()
    {
        $this->_init('mdg_giftregistry/type');
        parent::_construct();
    }
}
```

We will also need to create a resource class; every Magento Data model has its own resource class. It is also important to clarify that only models that handle the data directly, be it a simple data model or an EAV model, will require a `resource` class. To do so, follow these steps:

1. Navigate to the `Model` folder on our module directory.

2. Create a new folder under `Model` called `Mysql4`.

3. Create a new file called `Type.php` and copy the following content into the file (the file location is `app/code/local/Mdg/Giftregistry/Model/Mysql4/Type.php`):

```php
<?php
class Mdg_Giftregistry_Model_Mysql4_Type extends Mage_Core_Model_
Mysql4_Abstract
{
    public function _construct()
    {
        $this->_init('mdg_giftregistry/type', 'type_id');
    }
}
```

Finally, we will also need a `collection` class to retrieve all available event types:

1. Navigate to the `Model` folder on our module directory.

2. Create a new file called `Type.php` and copy the following content into the file (the file location is `app/code/local/Mdg/Giftregistry/Model/Mysql4/Type/Collection.php`):

```php
<?php
class Mdg_Giftregistry_Model_Mysql4_Type_Collection extends Mage_
Core_Model_Mysql4_Collection_Abstract
{
    public function _construct()
    {
        $this->_init('mdg_giftregistry/type');
        parent::_construct();
    }
}
```

Let's do the same by creating a model that handles the gift registry items. This model will hold all the relevant product information for the registry items. To do so, follow these steps:

1. Navigate to the `Model` folder on our module directory.

2. Create a new file called `Item.php` and copy the following content into the file (the file location is `app/code/local/Mdg/Giftregistry/Model/Item.php`):

```php
<?php
class Mdg_Giftregistry_Model_Item extends Mage_Core_Model_Abstract
{
    public function __construct()
    {
        $this->_init('mdg_giftregistry/item');
        parent::_construct();
    }
}
```

Let's go ahead and create the resource class:

1. Navigate to the `Model` folder on our module directory.

2. Open the `Mysql4` folder

3. Create a new file called `Item.php` and copy the following content into the file (the file location is `app/code/local/Mdg/Giftregistry/Model/Mysql4/Item.php`):

```php
<?php
class Mdg_Giftregistry_Model_Mysql4_Item extends Mage_Core_Model_Mysql4_Abstract
{
    public function _construct()
    {
        $this->_init('mdg_giftregistry/item', 'item_id');
    }
}
```

And, finally, let's create the corresponding `collection` class:

1. Navigate to the `Model` folder on our module directory.

2. Create a new file called `Collection.php` and copy the following content into the file (the file location is `app/code/local/Mdg/Giftregistry/Model/Mysql4/Item/Collection.php`):

```php
<?php
class Mdg_Giftregistry_Model_Mysql4_Item_Collection extends Mage_Core_Model_Mysql4_Collection_Abstract
```

```
{
    public function _construct()
    {
        $this->_init('mdg_giftregistry/item');
        parent::_construct();
    }
}
```

Our next step will be to create our Registry entity; this is the core of our registry and is the model that ties everything together. To do so, follow these steps:

1. Navigate to the `Model` folder on our module directory.

2. Create a new file called `Entity.php` and copy the following content into the file (the file location is `app/code/local/Mdg/Giftregistry/Model/Entity.php`):

```php
<?php
class Mdg_Giftregistry_Model_Entity extends Mage_Core_Model_Abstract
{
    public function __construct()
    {
        $this->_init('mdg_giftregistry/entity');
        parent::_construct();
    }
}
```

Let's go ahead and create the `resource` class:

1. Navigate to the `Model` folder on our module directory.

2. Open the `Mysql4` folder.

3. Create a new file called `Entity.php` and copy the following content into the file (the file location is `app/code/local/Mdg/Giftregistry/Model/Mysql4/Entity.php`):

```php
<?php
class Mdg_Giftregistry_Model_Mysql4_Entity extends Mage_Core_Model_Mysql4_Abstract
{
    public function _construct()
    {
        $this->_init('mdg_giftregistry/entity', 'entity_id');
    }
}
```

And, finally, let's create the corresponding `collection` class:

1. Navigate to the `Model` folder on our module directory.

2. Create a new file called `Collection.php` and copy the following content into the file (the file location is `app/code/local/Mdg/Giftregistry/Model/Mysql4/Entity/Collection.php`):

```php
<?php
class Mdg_Giftregistry_Model_Mysql4_Entity_Collection extends
Mage_Core_Model_Mysql4_Collection_Abstract
{
    public function _construct()
    {
        $this->_init('mdg_giftregistry/entity');
        parent::_construct();
    }
}
```

So far, we haven't done anything other than blindly creating new models by copying code and adding model classes to our module. Let's test our newly created models using the **Interactive Magento Console (IMC)**.

Let's fire up IMC and try out the new models by running the following command in the root of our Magento installation:

```
$ php shell/imc.php
```

The following code assumes that you are running a Magento test installation with sample data, and if you are using the Vagrant box installation, you already have all the preloaded data:

1. We will start by loading the customer model:

```
magento > $customer = Mage::getModel('customer/customer')-
>load(1);
```

2. Next we need to instantiate a new registry object:

```
magento > $registry = Mage::getModel('mdg_giftregistry/entity');
```

3. One handy function that is part of all Magento models is the `getData()` function, which returns an array of all the object attributes. Let's run this function on both a, the registry and customer object and compare the output:

```
magento > print_r($customer->getData());
```

```
magento > print_r($registry->getData());
```

4. As we notice, the customer has all the data set for our John Doe example record, while the registry object returns completely empty `$regiarray`. Let's change this by running the following code:

```
magento > $registry->setCustomerId($customer->getId());

magento > $registry->setTypeId(1);

magento > $registry->setWebsiteId(1);

magento > $registry->setEventDate('2012-12-12');

magento > $registry->setEventCountry('CA');

magento > $registry->setEventLocation('Toronto');
```

5. Now let's try to print the registry data one more time by running:

```
magento > print_r($registry->getData());
```

6. Finally, to make our changes permanent, we need to call the model `save` function:

```
magento > $registry->save();
```

And oops! Something went wrong when saving the product; we got the following error in the console:

```
Fatal error: Call to a member function beginTransaction() on a non-
object in .../app/code/core/Mage/Core/Model/Abstract.php on line 313
```

What happened? The `save()` function that is being called is part of the parent class `Mage_Core_Model_Mysql4_Abstract`, which in turn calls the abstract class `save()` function, but we are missing a critical part of our `config.xml` file.

In order for Magento to properly identify which resource class to use, we need to specify the resource model class and the matching table for each entity. Let's go ahead and update our configuration file by following these steps:

1. Navigate to the extension `etc/` folder.
2. Open `config.xml`.
3. Update the `<model>` node with the following code (the file location is `app/code/local/Mdg/Giftregistry/Model/Entity.php`):

```
...
<models>
    <mdg_giftregistry>
        <class>Mdg_Giftregistry_Model</class>
        <resourceModel>mdg_giftregistry_mysql4</resourceModel>
    </mdg_giftregistry>
```

```
<mdg_giftregistry_mysql4>
    <class>Mdg_Giftregistry_Model_Mysql4</class>
    <entities>
        <entity>
            <table>mdg_giftregistry_entity</table>
        </entity>
        <item>
            <table>mdg_giftregistry_item</table>
        </item>
        <type>
            <table>mdg_giftregistry_type</table>
        </type>
    </entities>
</mdg_giftregistry_mysql4>
</models>
...
```

Now, before we can actually save a product to the database, we have to create our database tables first; next, we will learn how to use setup resources for creating our table structures and setting our default data.

Setup resources

Now that we have created our model code, we need to create setup resources in order to be able to save them. The setup resources will take care of creating the corresponding database tables. Now, we could just use straight SQL or a tool such as PHPMyAdmin to create all the tables, but this is not the standard practice, and by general rule, we should never modify the Magento Database directly.

To achieve this, we will do the following:

- Define a setup resource on our configuration file
- Create a resource class
- Create an installer script
- Create a data script
- Create an upgrade script

Defining a setup resource

When we first defined our configuration file, we defined a `<resources>` node:

The file location is `app/code/local/Mdg/Giftregistry/etc/config.xml`. Refer to the following code snippet:

```
...
<resources>
    <mdg_giftregistry_setup>
        <setup>
            <module>Mdg_Giftregistry</module>
        </setup>
    </mdg_giftregistry_setup>
</resources>
...
```

The first thing to notice is that the `<mdg_giftregistry_setup>` node is used as a unique identifier for our setup resource; the standard naming convention is `<modulename_setup>`, and while it is not required, it is highly recommended to follow this naming convention.

We will also need to make a change to the `<setup>` node, add an additional class node, and read and write connections:

The file location is `app/code/local/Mdg/Giftregistry/etc/config.xml`.

```
...
<resources>
    <mdg_giftregistry_setup>
        <setup>
            <module>Mdg_Giftregistry</module>
            <class>Mdg_Giftregistry_Model_Resource_Setup</class>
        </setup>
        <connection>
            <use>core_setup</use>
        </connection>
    </mdg_giftregistry_setup>
    <mdg_giftregistry_write>
        <connection>
            <use>core_write</use>
        </connection>
    </mdg_giftregistry_write>
    <mdg_giftregistry_read>
        <connection>
            <use>core_read</use>
```

```
        </connection>
      </mdg_giftregistry_read>
  </resources>
  ...
```

Creating this setup resource is not required for the basic setup scripts, and `Mage_Core_Model_Resource_Setup` can be used instead, but by creating our own setup class, we are planning ahead and giving ourselves more flexibility for future improvements. Next, we will create the setup resource class under the file location, otherwise we will be getting an error saying that Magento can't find the setup resource class.

Create the setup resource class under the file location, `app/code/local/Mdg/Giftregistry/Model/Resource/Setup.php`. Refer to the following code snippet:

```php
<?php
class Mdg_Giftregistry_Model_Resource_Setup extends Mage_Core_Model_
Resource_Setup
{

}
```

For now, we don't need to do anything else with the setup resource class.

Creating the Installer Script

Our next step will be to create an installation script. This script contains all the SQL code for creating our tables and is run when we initialize our module. First, let's take another quick look to our `config.xml` file. If we remember, the first node defined before our `<global>` node was the `<modules>` node.

The file location is `app/code/local/Mdg/Giftregistry/etc/config.xml`. Refer to the following code snippet:

```xml
<modules>
  <Mdg_Giftregistry>
      <version>0.1.0</version>
  </Mdg_Giftregistry>
</modules>
```

As we mentioned before, this node is required on all Magento modules and is used to identify the current installed version of our module. This version number is used by Magento to identify if and which installation and upgrade scripts to run.

A word on naming conventions: Since Magento 1.6, the setup script naming conventions have changed. Originally, the `Mysql4-install-x.x.x.php` naming convention was used and is currently deprecated but still supported.

Since Magento 1.6, the naming convention for the setup script has changed and now developers can make use of three different script types:

- **Install**: This script is used when the module is first installed and no record of it exists on the `core_resource` table

- **Upgrade**: This script is used if the version in the `core_resource` table is lower than the one in the `config.xml` file

- **Data**: This script will run after the matching version install/upgrade script and are used to populate the tables with required data

 Data script are introduced in Magento 1.6 and are stored under the data/directory directly under our Module root. They follow a slightly different convention than the install and upgrade scripts by adding the prefix.

Let's continue creating our registry entity table in our installation script under.

The file location is `app/code/local/Mdg/Giftregistry/sql/mdg_giftregistry_setup/install-0.1.0.php`. Refer to the following code:

```php
<?php

$installer = $this;
$installer->startSetup();
// Create the mdg_giftregistry/registry table
$tableName = $installer->getTable('mdg_giftregistry/entity');
// Check if the table already exists
if ($installer->getConnection()->isTableExists($tableName) != true) {
    $table = $installer->getConnection()
        ->newTable($tableName)
        ->addColumn('entity_id', Varien_Db_Ddl_Table::TYPE_INTEGER,
null,
            array(
                'identity' => true,
                'unsigned' => true,
                'nullable' => false,
                'primary' => true,
            ),
```

```
                    'Entity Id'
            )
            ->addColumn('customer_id', Varien_Db_Ddl_Table::TYPE_INTEGER,
null,
                array(
                    'unsigned' => true,
                    'nullable' => false,
                    'default' => '0',
                ),
                'Customer Id'
            )
            ->addColumn('type_id', Varien_Db_Ddl_Table::TYPE_SMALLINT,
null,
                array(
                    'unsigned' => true,
                    'nullable' => false,
                    'default' => '0',
                ),
                'Type Id'
            )
            ->addColumn('website_id', Varien_Db_Ddl_Table::TYPE_SMALLINT,
null,
                array(
                    'unsigned' => true,
                    'nullable' => false,
                    'default' => '0',
                ),
                'Website Id'
            )
            ->addColumn('event_name', Varien_Db_Ddl_Table::TYPE_TEXT, 255,
                array(),
                'Event Name'
            )
            ->addColumn('event_date', Varien_Db_Ddl_Table::TYPE_DATE,
null,
                array(),
                'Event Date'
            )
            ->addColumn('event_country', Varien_Db_Ddl_Table::TYPE_TEXT,
3,
                array(),
                'Event Country'
            )
            ->addColumn('event_location', Varien_Db_Ddl_Table::TYPE_TEXT,
255,
```

```
                array(),
                'Event Location'
            )
        ->addColumn('created_at', Varien_Db_Ddl_Table::TYPE_TIMESTAMP,
null,
            array(
                'nullable' => false,
            ),
            'Created At')
        ->addIndex($installer->getIdxName('mdg_giftregistry/entity',
array('customer_id')),
            array('customer_id'))
        ->addIndex($installer->getIdxName('mdg_giftregistry/entity',
array('website_id')),
            array('website_id'))
        ->addIndex($installer->getIdxName('mdg_giftregistry/entity',
array('type_id')),
            array('type_id'))
        ->addForeignKey(
            $installer->getFkName(
                'mdg_giftregistry/entity',
                'customer_id',
                'customer/entity',
                'entity_id'
            ),
            'customer_id', $installer->getTable('customer/entity'),
'entity_id',
            Varien_Db_Ddl_Table::ACTION_CASCADE, Varien_Db_Ddl_
Table::ACTION_CASCADE)
        ->addForeignKey(
            $installer->getFkName(
                'mdg_giftregistry/entity',
                'website_id',
                'core/website',
                'website_id'
            ),
            'website_id', $installer->getTable('core/website'),
'website_id',
            Varien_Db_Ddl_Table::ACTION_CASCADE, Varien_Db_Ddl_
Table::ACTION_CASCADE)
        ->addForeignKey(
            $installer->getFkName(
```

```
                'mdg_giftregistry/entity',
                'type_id',
                'mdg_giftregistry/type',
                'type_id'
            ),
            'type_id', $installer->getTable('mdg_giftregistry/type'),
'type_id',
            Varien_Db_Ddl_Table::ACTION_CASCADE, Varien_Db_Ddl_
Table::ACTION_CASCADE);

    $installer->getConnection()->createTable($table);
}
$installer->endSetup();
```

> Please note that due to space constraints we are not adding the full installation script; you still need to add the installer code for the item and type tables. The full installation file and the code files can be downloaded directly from `https://github.com/amacgregor/mdg_giftreg`.

Now that might look like a lot of code, but it is only creating one output of the tables, in order to make sense of it, lets break it down, and see what is exactly the code doing.

The first thing to notice is that even if we are creating and setting database tables, we are not writing any SQL code. Magento ORM provides an adapter with the database. All the installation, upgrade, and data scripts inherit from `Mage_Core_Model_Resource_Setup`. Let's break down each of the functions being used on our installation script.

The first three lines of the script instantiate both `resource_setup` model and the connection. The rest of the script deals with setting up a new table instance and calling the following functions on it:

- `addColumn`: This function is used to define each of the table columns and takes the following five parameters:
    ◦ `name`: This is the name of the column
    ◦ `type`: This is the data storage type (`int`, `varchar`, `text`, and so on)
    ◦ `size`: This is the column length
    ◦ `options`: This is an array of additional options for the data storage
    ◦ `Comment`: This is the column description

- `addIndex`: This function is used to define the indexes of a particular table and takes the following three parameters:
  - ° `index`: This is an index name
  - ° `columns`: This can be a string with a single column name or an array with multiple ones
  - ° `options`: This is an array of additional options for the data storage
- `addForeginKey`: This function is used to define foreign key relationships, and it takes the following six parameters:
  - ° `fkName`: This is a foreign key name
  - ° `column`: This is a foreign key column name
  - ° `refTable`: This is a reference table name
  - ° `refColumn`: This is a reference table column name
  - ° `onDelete`: This is an action to take on delete row
  - ° `onUpdate`: This is an action to take on update of row

The code creating each of our tables is basically composed of those three functions, and after each table definition, the following code is executed:

```
$installer->getConnection()->createTable($table);
```

This is telling our database adapter to convert our code into SQL and run it against the database. There is one important thing to notice; that is, instead of providing or hard-coding the database names, the following code is called:

```
$installer->getTable('mdg_giftregistry/entity')
```

This is the table alias that we defined before inside our `config.xml` files. To finish our installer, we need to create a `newTable` instance for each of our entities.

 Here's a challenge for you. Create the missing tables by using your Installer Script. To see the answer with the complete code and full breakdown, visit `http://www.magedevguide.com/challenge/chapter4/1`.

The data scripts can be used to populate our tables; in our case, this will come in handy to set up some base event types.

We will first need to create a data installation script under the data folder; as we mentioned before, the structure is very similar to the SQL folder, and the only difference is that we append the data prefix to the matching installation/upgrade script. To do so, follow these steps:

1. Navigate to the module data folder app/code/local/Mdg/Giftregistry/data/.

2. Create a new directory based on resource; in this case, it would be mdg_giftregistry_setup.

3. Under mdg_giftregistry_setup, create a file called data-install-0.1.0.php.

4. Copy the following code into the data-install-0.1.0.php file (the file location is app/code/local/Mdg/Giftregistry/data/mdg_giftregistry_setup/data-install-0.1.0.php):

```php
<?php
$registryTypes = array(
    array(
        'code' => 'baby_shower',
        'name' => 'Baby Shower',
        'description' => 'Baby Shower',
        'store_id' => Mage_Core_Model_App::ADMIN_STORE_ID,
        'is_active' => 1,
    ),
    array(
        'code' => 'wedding',
        'name' => 'Wedding',
        'description' => 'Wedding',
        'store_id' => Mage_Core_Model_App::ADMIN_STORE_ID,
        'is_active' => 1,
    ),
    array(
        'code' => 'birthday',
        'name' => 'Birthday',
        'description' => 'Birthday',
        'store_id' => Mage_Core_Model_App::ADMIN_STORE_ID,
        'is_active' => 1,
    ),
);

foreach ($registryTypes as $data) {
    Mage::getModel('mdg_giftregistry/type')
        ->addData($data)
        ->setStoreId($data['store_id'])
        ->save();
}
```

Let's take a closer look at the last conditional block on the `data-install-0.1.0.php` script:

```
foreach ($registryTypes as $data) {
    Mage::getModel('mdg_giftregistry/type')
        ->addData($data)
        ->setStoreId($data['store_id'])
        ->save();
}
```

Now, if we refresh our Magento installation, the error should be gone, and if we take a close look at the `mdg_giftregistry_type` table, we should see the following records:

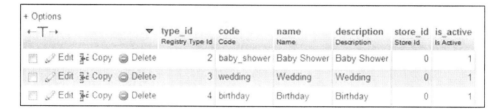

As we learned before, the installation and data scripts will run the first time our module is installed. But what happens in our case where Magento already thinks our module is installed?

Since the module is already registered in the `core_resource` table, the installation scripts will not be run again, unless Magento detects a version change in the extension. This is great for handling multiple releases of an extension but not very practical for development purposes.

Fortunately, it is easy to trick Magento into running our extension installation scripts again. We only have to delete the corresponding entry in the `core_resource` table. To do so, follow these steps:

1. Open your MySQL console; if you are using our Vagrant box, you can just open it by typing `mysql`.
2. Once we are in the MySQL shell, we need to select our working database; in our case, it is `ce1702_magento`.
3. Finally, we need to enter the `core_resource` table using the following query:

   ```
   mysql> DELETE FROM `core_resource` WHERE `code` = 'mdg_
   giftregistry_setup'
   ```

What have we learned?

So far, we have learned to:

- Create the base directory structure for our Magento module
- The role and importance of the configuration files
- Creating models and setup resources
- The role and order of installation, upgrade, and data scripts

 Here's a challenge for you. Try improving the model structure for our module even further by converting the entity into an EAV model; this will require modifications to the installation scripts and to the resource model. To see the answer with the complete code and full breakdown, visit `http://www.magedevguide.com/challenge/chapter4/2`.

Setting up our routes

Now that we are capable of saving and manipulating the data by using our models, we need to provide a way for customers to interact with the actual gift registries; that is our first step. We need to create valid routes or URLs in the frontend.

As with many things in Magento, this is controlled by the configuration file. A route will convert a URL into a valid controller, action, and method.

Open our `config.xml` file. The file location is `app/code/local/Mdg/Giftregistry/etc/config.xml`. Refer to the following code:

```
<config>
...
    <frontend>
        <routers>
            <mdg_giftregistry>
                <use>standard</use>
                <args>
                    <module>Mdg_Giftregistry</module>
                    <frontName>giftregistry</frontName>
                </args>
            </mdg_giftregistry>
        </routers>
    </frontend>
...
</config>
```

Let's break down the configuration code we just added:

- `<frontend>`: Previously, we added all the configuration inside the global scope; since we want our routes to be only available in the frontend, we need to declare our custom routes under the frontend scope
- `<routers>`: This is the container tag that holds the configuration for our custom routes
- `<mdg_giftregistry>`: The naming convention for this tag is to match the module name and is the unique identifier for our route
- `<frontName>`: As we learned in *Chapter 2*, *Magento Fundamentals for Developers*, Magento breaks down the URLs into `http://localhost.com /frontName/actionControllerName/actionMethod/`.

Once we have defined our route configuration, we need to create an actual controller to handle all the incoming requests.

The index controller

Our first step is to create `IndexController` under our module controllers directory. Magento will always try to load `IndexController` if no controller name is specified.

The file location is `app/code/local/Mdg/Giftregistry/controllers/Index.php`. Refer to the following code:

```php
<?php
class Mdg_Giftregistry_IndexController extends Mage_Core_Controller_
Front_Action
{
    public function indexAction()
  {
    echo 'This is our test controller';
      }
}
```

After creating our file, if we go to `http://localhost.com/giftregistry/index/index`, we should see a blank page with a message saying, **This is our test controller**. This is because we are not properly loading the layout of our customer controller. The file location is `app/code/local/Mdg/Giftregistry/controllers/IndexController.php`. We need to change our action code to:

```php
<?php
class Mdg_Giftregistry_IndexController extends Mage_Core_Controller_
Front_Action
{
```

```
   public function indexAction()
 {
   $this->loadLayout();
   $this->renderLayout();
     }
 }
```

Before going into the details of what is happening within the controller action; let's create the rest of the controllers and corresponding actions.

We will need a controller that takes care of the basic operations for customers so they are able to create, manage, and delete their registries. Also, we will require a search controller so family and friends can locate the matching gift registries, and finally, we will require a view controller for showing the registry details.

Our first step will be to add the remaining actions to the index controller (the file location is `app/code/local/Mdg/Giftregistry/controllers/IndexController.php`):

```php
<?php
class Mdg_Giftregistry_IndexController extends Mage_Core_Controller_
Front_Action
{
    public function indexAction()
    {
        $this->loadLayout();
        $this->renderLayout();
        return $this;
    }

    public function deleteAction()
    {
        $this->loadLayout();
        $this->renderLayout();
        return $this;
    }

    public function newAction()
    {
        $this->loadLayout();
        $this->renderLayout();
        return $this;
    }

    public function editAction()
```

```
    {
        $this->loadLayout();
        $this->renderLayout();
        return $this;
    }

    public function newPostAction()
    {
        $this->loadLayout();
        $this->renderLayout();
        return $this;
    }

    public function editPostAction()
    {
        $this->loadLayout();
        $this->renderLayout();
        return $this;
    }
}
```

Before we start adding all the logic to the index controller, we need to take an extra step to prevent not logged in customers to access the giftregistry functionality. Magento Front Controller is already very useful for handling this; it's called the preDispatch() function, which is executed before any other action in the controller.

Open your IndexController.php and add the following code at the beginning of the class.

The file location is app/code/local/Mdg/Giftregistry/controllers/ IndexController.php. Refer to the following code:

```
<?php
class Mdg_Giftregistry_IndexController extends Mage_Core_Controller_
Front_Action
{
    public function preDispatch()
    {
        parent::preDispatch();
        if (!Mage::getSingleton('customer/session')-
>authenticate($this)) {
            $this->getResponse()->setRedirect(Mage::helper('custom
er')->getLoginUrl());
            $this->setFlag('', self::FLAG_NO_DISPATCH, true);
        }
    }
    ...
```

Now, if we try to load `http://localhost.com/giftregistry/index/index`, we will be redirected to the login page unless we are logged in to the frontend.

Our next step will be to add all the logic to each of the controller actions so the controller can properly handle creation, update, and deletion.

The index, new, and edit actions are mostly used to load and render the layout, so there is not much logic involved in controller, `newPostAction()`, `editPostAction()`, and `deleteAction()`; on the other hand, they handle a heavier and more complicated logic.

Let's get started with `newPostAction()`. This action is used to handle the data received from the `newAction()` form. To do so, follow these steps:

1. Open `IndexController.php`.

2. The first thing we will add to the action is an `if` statement to check if the request is a post-request, which we can retrieve by using the following code:

   ```
   $this->getRequest()->isPost()
   ```

3. In addition to that, we also want to check that the request has actual data; for that, we can use the following code:

   ```
   $this->getRequest()->getParams()
   ```

Once we have validated that, the request is a proper request, and while we are receiving data, we need to actually create gift registry. To do so, we will add a new function inside our registry model by following these steps:

1. Open the registry entity model.

2. Create a new function called `updateRegistryData()` and make sure the function takes two parameters: `$customer` and `$data`.

3. The file location is `app/code/local/Mdg/Giftregistry/Model/Entity.php`. Add the following code inside this function:

   ```php
   public function updateRegistryData(Mage_Customer_Model_Customer
   $customer, $data)
   {
       try{
           if(!empty($data))
           {
               $this->setCustomerId($customer->getId());
               $this->setWebsiteId($customer->getWebsiteId());
               $this->setTypeId($data['type_id']);
               $this->setEventName($data['event_name']);
               $this->setEventDate($data['event_date']);
               $this->setEventCountry($data['event_country']);
   ```

```
                    $this->setEventLocation($data['event_location']);
            }else{
                    throw new Exception("Error Processing Request:
    Insufficient Data Provided");
            }
        } catch (Exception $e){
            Mage::logException($e);
        }
        return $this;
    }
```

This function will help us out by adding the form data into the current instance of the registry object, which means we need to create one inside our controller. Let's put the code for our controller together:

The file location is app/code/local/Mdg/Giftregistry/controllers/ IndexController.php. Refer to the following code snippet:

```
public function newPostAction()
{
    try {
        $data = $this->getRequest()->getParams();
        $registry = Mage::getModel('mdg_giftregistry/entity');
        $customer = Mage::getSingleton('customer/session')-
>getCustomer();

        if($this->getRequest()->getPost() && !empty($data)) {
            $registry->updateRegistryData($customer, $data);
            $registry->save();
            $successMessage = Mage::helper('mdg_giftregistry')->__
('Registry Successfully Created');
            Mage::getSingleton('core/session')-
>addSuccess($successMessage);
        }else{
            throw new Exception("Insufficient Data provided");
        }
    } catch (Mage_Core_Exception $e) {
        Mage::getSingleton('core/session')->addError($e-
>getMessage());
        $this->_redirect('*/*/');
    }
    $this->_redirect('*/*/');
}
```

We have created a very basic controller action that will handle the registry creation and that will handle most of the possible exceptions.

Let's continue by creating `editPostAction`; this action is very similar to the `newPostAction`. The main difference is that in the case of `editPostAction`, we are working with an already existing registry record, so we will need to add some validation before setting the data.

The file location is `app/code/local/Mdg/Giftregistry/controllers/IndexController.php`. Let's take a closer look at the following action code:

```
public function editPostAction()
{
    try {
        $data = $this->getRequest()->getParams();
        $registry = Mage::getModel('mdg_giftregistry/entity');
        $customer = Mage::getSingleton('customer/session')-
>getCustomer();

        if($this->getRequest()->getPosts() && !empty($data) )
        {
            $registry->load($data['registry_id']);
            if($registry){
                $registry->updateRegistryData($customer, $data);
                $registry->save();
                $successMessage =  Mage::helper('mdg_
giftregistry')->__('Registry Successfully Saved');
                Mage::getSingleton('core/session')-
>addSuccess($successMessage);
            }else {
                throw new Exception("Invalid Registry Specified");
            }
        }else {
            throw new Exception("Insufficient Data provided");
        }
    } catch (Mage_Core_Exception $e) {
        Mage::getSingleton('core/session')->addError($e-
>getMessage());
        $this->_redirect('*/*/');
    }
    $this->_redirect('*/*/');
}
```

As we can see, this code is pretty much the same as our `newPostAction()` controller with the critical distinction that it tries to load an existing registry before updating the data.

Here's a challenge for you. Since the code between
`editPostAction()` and `newPostAction()` are very similar,
try combining both into a single post action that can be reused. To
see the answer with the complete code and full breakdown, visit
`http://www.magedevguide.com/challenge/chapter4/3`.

To finalize `IndexController`, we need to add an action that allows us to delete a
specific registry record; for that, we will use `deleteAction()`.

Thanks to the Magento ORM system, this process is really simple, as Magento
models inherit the `delete()` function, which as the name implies will simply
delete that specific model instance.

The file location is `app/code/local/Mdg/Giftregistry/controllers/`
`IndexController.php`. Inside `IndexController`, add the following code:

```
public function deleteAction()
{
    try {
        $registryId = $this->getRequest()->getParam('registry_id');
        if($registryId && $this->getRequest()->getPost()){
            if($registry = Mage::getModel('mdg_giftregistry/entity')-
>load($registryId))
            {
                $registry->delete();
                $successMessage =  Mage::helper('mdg_
giftregistry')->__('Gift registry has been succesfully deleted.');
                Mage::getSingleton('core/session')-
>addSuccess($successMessage);
            }else{
                throw new Exception("There was a problem deleting the
registry");
            }
        }
    } catch (Exception $e) {
        Mage::getSingleton('core/session')->addError($e-
>getMessage());
        $this->_redirect('*/*/');
    }
}
```

The important actions to notice in our delete controller are as follows:

1. We check for the right type of request into our action.
2. We instantiate the registry object and verify if it is a valid one.
3. Finally, we call the `delete()` function on the registry instance.

You might notice by now that since we have made a critical omission, there is no way to add an actual product to our cart.

We will be skipping that particular action for now, and we will create it after we have a better understanding of the blocks and layouts involved and how it interacts with our custom controllers.

The search controller

Now that we have a working `IndexController` that will handle most of the logic for modifying actual registries, the next controller that we will create is `SearchController`. To do so, follow these steps:

1. Create a new controller under the controllers directory with the name `SearchController`.

2. The file location is `app/code/local/Mdg/Giftregistry/controllers/SearchController.php`. Copy the following code into the search controller:

```php
<?php
class Mdg_Giftregistry_SearchController extends Mage_Core_
Controller_Front_Action
{
    public function indexAction()
    {
        $this->loadLayout();
        $this->renderLayout();
        return $this;
    }
    public function resultsAction()
    {
        $this->loadLayout();
        $this->renderLayout();
        return $this;
    }
}
```

We will leave `indexAction` for now, and we will focus on the logic involved in `resultsAction()`, which will be taking the search parameters and loading a registry collection.

The file location is `app/code/local/Mdg/Giftregistry/controllers/ SearchController.php`. Let's take a look at the complete action code and break it down:

```php
public function resultsAction()
{
    $this->loadLayout();
    if ($searchParams = $this->getRequest()->getParam('search_
params')) {
        $results = Mage::getModel('mdg_giftregistry/entity')-
>getCollection();
        if($searchParams['type']){
            $results->addFieldToFilter('type_id',
$searchParams['type']);
        }
        if($searchParams['date']){
            $results->addFieldToFilter('event_date',
$searchParams['date']);
        }
        if($searchParams['location']){
            $results->addFieldToFilter('event_location',
$searchParams['location']);
        }
        $this->getLayout()->getBlock('mdg_giftregistry.search.
results')
            ->setResults($results);
    }
    $this->renderLayout();
    return $this;
}
```

As with previous actions, we are taking the request parameters, but in this particular case, we load a gift registry collection and apply a field filter for each of the available fields. One thing to stand out is that this is the first time we are interacting with the layout directly from a Magento controller.

```php
$this->getLayout()->getBlock('mdg_giftregistry.search.results')

    ->setResults($results);
```

What we are doing here is making the loaded registry collection available to that particular block instance.

The view controller

Finally, we need a controller that allows displaying registry details regardless of whether a customer is logged in or not. Follow these steps:

1. Create a new controller under the controllers directory with the name `ViewController`.

2. Open the controller that we just created and refer to the following placeholder code (the file location is `app/code/local/Mdg/Giftregistry/controllers/ViewController.php`):

```php
<?php
class Mdg_Giftregistry_ViewController extends Mage_Core_Controller_Front_Action
{
    public function viewAction()
    {
        $registryId = $this->getRequest()->getParam('registry_id');
        if($registryId){
            $entity = Mage::getModel('mdg_giftregistry/entity');
            if($entity->load($registryId))
            {
                Mage::register('loaded_registry', $entity);
                $this->loadLayout();
                $this->_initLayoutMessages('customer/session');
                $this->renderLayout();
                return $this;
            } else {
                $this->_forward('noroute');
                return $this;
            }
        }
    }
}
```

So here we are using a new function, `Mage::register()`, which is setting a global variable that we can later retrieve into the application flow by any method. This function is part of the Magento Registry pattern that is compromised of the following three functions:

- `Mage::register()`: This function is used to set global variables
- `Mage::unregister()`: This function is used to unset global variables
- `Mage::registry()`: This function is used to retrieve global variables

We are using the registry function in this case to provide access to the registry entity further ahead the application flow and particularly in the view block that we will be creating next.

Block and layouts

As we learned in *Chapter 2*, *Magento Fundamentals for Developers*, Magento separates its view layer into blocks, templates, and layout files. Blocks are objects that handle parts of the logic. Templates are `phtml` files that are a mix of HTML and PHP code. Layout files are XML files that control the position of blocks.

Each module has its own layout file that is in charge of updating that specific module layout. We need to start by creating a layout file for our module by following these steps:

1. Navigate to `app/design/frontend/base/default/layout/`.
2. Create a file named `mdg_giftregistry.xml`.
3. Add the following code (the file location is `app/design/frontend/base/default/layout/mdg_giftregistry.xml`):

```
<layout version="0.1.0">
  <mdg_giftregistry_index_index>
  </mdg_giftregistry_index_index>

  <mdg_giftregistry_index_new>
  </mdg_giftregistry_index_new>

  <mdg_giftregistry_index_edit>
  </mdg_giftregistry_index_edit>

  <mdg_giftregistry_view_view>
  </mdg_giftregistry_view_view>

  <mdg_giftregistry_search_index>
  </mdg_giftregistry_search_index>

  <mdg_giftregistry_search_results>
  </mdg_giftregistry_search_results>
</layout>
```

 Note that by adding our templates and layouts to the base/default theme, we'll make our templates and layouts available to all stores and themes.

If we take a closer look at the XML we just pasted, we can see that we have a default `<xml>` tag and several other sets of tags. As we mentioned earlier, in Magento, routes are formed by a frontend name, a controller, and an action.

Each of the XML tags in the layout file represents one of our controllers and actions; for example, `<giftregistry_index_index>` will control the layout of our `IndexController` action; Magento assigns each page a unique handle.

In order for Magento to recognize our layout file, we need to declare the layout file inside the `config.xml` file by following these steps:

1. Navigate to the `extension etc/` folder.

2. Open `config.xml`.

3. Add the following code inside the `<frontend>` node (the file location is `app/design/frontend/base/default/layout/mdg_giftregistry.xml`):

```
<frontend>
    <layout>
        <updates>
            <mdg_giftregistry module="mdg_giftregistry">
                <file>mdg_giftregistry.xml</file>
            </mdg_giftregistry>
        </updates>
    </layout>
    ...
</frontend>
```

IndexController blocks and views

As we did before, we will start by building the index controller. Let's define which templates and blocks we need to define for each of the actions:

- **Index**: This is the list of the current customer available registries
- **New**: This provides a new form to capture the registry information
- **Edit**: This loads a specific registry data and loads them in the form

For the index action, we will need to create a new block called `List.php`. Let's start by creating the registry list block by following these steps:

1. Navigate to `app/code/local/Mdg/Giftregistry/Block/`.

2. Create a file named `List.php`.

3. Copy the following code (the file location is `app/code/local/Mdg/Giftregistry/Block/List.php.`):

```php
<?php
class Mdg_Giftregistry_Block_list extends Mage_Core_Block_Template
{
    public function getCustomerRegistries()
    {
        $collection = null;
        $currentCustomer = Mage::getSingleton('customer/session')-
>getCustomer();
        if($currentCustomer)
        {
            $collection = Mage::getModel('mdg_giftregistry/
entity')->getCollection()
                    ->addFieldToFilter('customer_id',
$currentCustomer->getId());
        }
        return $collection;
    }
}
```

The previous code declares our list block that will be used in `IndexController`. The blocks declares the `getCustomerRegistries()` method, which will check for the current customer and try to retrieve a collection of registries based on that customer.

Now that we created a new block, we need to add it to our layout XML file:

1. Open `mdg_giftregistry.xml`.
2. Add the following code inside `<mdg_gifregistry_index_index>` (the file location is `app/design/frontend/base/default/layout/mdg_giftregistry.xml`):

```xml
<reference name="content">
    <block name="giftregistry.list" type="mdg_giftregistry/list"
template="mdg/list.phtml" as="giftregistry_list"/>
</reference>
```

In the layout, we are declaring our block; inside that declaration, we are setting the block name, template, and type. If we try loading the index controller page right now, since we have not created our template file, we should then see an error about the missing template.

Let's create the template file:

1. Navigate to `design/frontend/base/default/template/`.
2. Create the `mdg/` folder.
3. Inside that folder, create a file called `list.phtml` (the file location is `app/design/frontend/base/default/template/mdg/list.phtml`):

```
<?php
$_collection = $this->getCustomerRegistries();
?>
<div class="customer-list">
    <ul>
        <?php foreach($_collection as $registry): ?>
            <li>
                <h3><?php echo $registry->getEventName(); ?></h3>
                <p><strong><?php echo $this->__('Event Date:') ?>
<?php echo $registry->getEventDate(); ?></strong></p>
                <p><strong><?php echo $this->__('Event Location:')
?> <?php echo $registry->getEventLocation(); ?></strong></p>
                <a href="<?php echo $this->getUrl('giftregistry/
view/view', array('_query' => array('registry_id' => $registry-
>getEntityId())))  ?>">
                    <?php echo $this->__('View Registry') ?>
                </a>
            </li>
        <?php endforeach; ?>
    </ul>
</div>
```

This is the first time we generate a .phtml file. As we mentioned before, .phtml files are just a combination of PHP and HTML code.

In case of the `list.phtml` file, the first thing we are doing is to load a collection by calling the `getCustomerRegistries()` method; one thing to notice is that we are actually calling `$this->getCustomerRegistries()`, as each template is assigned to a specific block.

We are missing a couple of important things, which are as follows:

*   If there are no registries for the current customer, we would only display an empty unordered list
*   There is no link to delete or edit a specific registry

One quick way of checking if the collection has registries is to call the `count` function and display an error message if the collection is actually empty.

The file location is `app/design/frontend/base/default/template/mdg/list.phtml`. Refer to the following code:

```php
<?php
    $_collection = $this->getCustomerRegistries();
?>
<div class="customer-list">
    <?php if (!$_collection->count()): ?>
        <h2><?php echo $this->__('You have no registries.') ?></h2>
        <a href="<?php echo $this->getUrl('giftregistry/index/new')
?>">
            <?php echo $this->__('Click Here to create a new Gift
Registry') ?>
        </a>
    <?php else: ?>
        <ul>
            <?php foreach($_collection as $registry): ?>
                <li>
                    <h3><?php echo $registry->getEventName(); ?></h3>
                    <p><strong><?php echo $this->__('Event Date:') ?>
<?php echo $registry->getEventDate(); ?></strong></p>
                    <p><strong><?php echo $this->__('Event Location:')
?> <?php echo $registry->getEventLocation(); ?></strong></p>
                    <a href="<?php echo $this->getUrl('giftregistry/
view/view', array('_query' => array('registry_id' => $registry-
>getEntityId())))) ?>">
                        <?php echo $this->__('View Registry') ?>
                    </a>
                    <a href="<?php echo $this->getUrl('giftregistry/
index/edit', array('_query' => array('registry_id' => $registry-
>getEntityId())))) ?>">
                        <?php echo $this->__('Edit Registry') ?>
                    </a>
                    <a href="<?php echo $this->getUrl('giftregistry/
index/delete', array('_query' => array('registry_id' => $registry-
>getEntityId())))) ?>">
                        <?php echo $this->__('Delete Registry') ?>
                    </a>

                </li>
            <?php endforeach; ?>
        </ul>
    <?php endif; ?>
</div>
```

We have added a new `if` statement to check that the collection count is not empty and a link to the `IndexController` edit action. Finally, if there are no registries to show, we are displaying an error message linking to the new action.

Let's continue by adding the block and templates for the new action:

1. Open the `mdg_giftregistry.xml` layout file.
2. Add the following code inside the `<mdg_gifregistry_index_new>` node (the file location is `app/design/frontend/base/default/layout/mdg_giftregistry.xml`):

```
<reference name="content">
    <block name="giftregistry.new" type="core/template"
template="mdg/new.phtml" as="giftregistry_new"/>
</reference>
```

Since we are just displaying a form to post the registry information to `newPostAction()`, we are just creating a core/template block with the custom template file that will contain the form code. Our template file will look like the following code.

The file location is `app/design/frontend/base/default/template/mdg/new.phtml`:

```
<?php $helper = Mage::helper('mdg_giftregistry'); ?>
<form action="<?php echo $this->getUrl('giftregistry/index/newPost/')
?>" method="post" id="form-validate">
    <fieldset>
        <?php echo $this->getBlockHtml('formkey')?>
        <ul class="form-list">
            <li>
                <label for="type_id"><?php echo $this->__('Event
type') ?></label>
                <select name="type_id" id="type_id">
                    <?php foreach($helper->getEventTypes() as $type):
?>
                        <option id="<?php echo $type->getTypeId(); ?>"
value="<?php echo $type->getCode(); ?>">
                            <?php echo $type->getName(); ?>
                        </option>
                    <?php endforeach; ?>
                </select>
            </li>
            <li class="field">
                <input type="text" name="event_name" id="event_name"
value="" title="Event Name"/>
```

```
                <label class="giftreg" for="event_name"><?php echo
$this->__('Event Name') ?></label>
            </li>
            <li class="field">
                <input type="text" name="event_location" id="event_
location" value="" title="Event Location"/>
                <label class="giftreg" for="event_location"><?php echo
$this->__('Event Location') ?></label>
            </li>
            <li class="field">
                <input type="text" name="event_country" id="event_
country" value="" title="Event Country"/>
                <label class="giftreg" for="event_country"><?php echo
$this->__('Event Country') ?></label>
            </li>
        </ul>
        <div class="buttons-set">
            <button type="submit" title="Save" class="button">
                <span>
                    <span><?php echo $this->__('Save') ?></span>
                </span>
            </button>
        </div>
    </fieldset>
</form>
<script type="text/javascript">
    //<![CDATA[
    var dataForm = new VarienForm('form-validate', true);
    //]]>
</script>
```

This time we are doing something new here. We are calling a helper; a helper is a class that contains methods that can be reused from blocks, templates, controllers, and so on. In our case, we are creating a helper that will retrieve all available registry types. Follow these steps:

1. Navigate to `app/code/local/Mdg/Giftregistry/Helper`.
2. Open the `Data.php` class.

3. Add the following code inside it (the file location is `app/code/local/Mdg/Giftregistry/Helper/Data.php`):

```php
<?php
class Mdg_Giftregistry_Helper_Data extends Mage_Core_Helper_
Abstract {

public function getEventTypes()
    {
        $collection = Mage::getModel('mdg_giftregistry/type')-
>getCollection();
        return $collection;
    }
}
```

Finally, we need to set up the edit template; the edit template will be exactly the same as the new template but with one major difference. We will check for the existence of a loaded registry and prepopulate the values of our fields.

The file location is `app/design/frontend/base/default/template/mdg/edit.phtml`. Refer to the following code:

```php
<?php
    $helper = Mage::helper('mdg_giftregistry');
    $loadedRegistry = Mage::getSingleton('customer/session')-
>getLoadedRegistry();
?>
<?php if($loadedRegistry): ?>
    <form action="<?php echo $this->getUrl('giftregistry/index/
editPost/') ?>" method="post" id="form-validate">
        <fieldset>
            <?php echo $this->getBlockHtml('formkey')?>
            <input type="hidden" id="type_id" value="<?php echo
$loadedRegistry->getTypeId(); ?>" />
            <ul class="form-list">
                <li class="field">
                    <label class="giftreg" for="event_name"><?php echo
$this->__('Event Name') ?></label>
                    <input type="text" name="event_name" id="event_
name" value="<?php echo $loadedRegistry->getEventName(); ?>"
title="Event Name"/>
                </li>
                <li class="field">
                    <label class="giftreg" for="event_location"><?php
echo $this->__('Event Location') ?></label>
```

```
                    <input type="text" name="event_location"
    id="event_location" value="<?php echo $loadedRegistry-
    >getEventLocation(); ?>" title="Event Location"/>
                </li>
                <li class="field">
                    <label class="giftreg" for="event_country"><?php
    echo $this->__('Event Country') ?></label>
                    <input type="text" name="event_country" id="event_
    country" value="<?php echo $loadedRegistry->getEventCountry(); ?>"
    title="Event Country"/>
                </li>
            </ul>
            <div class="buttons-set">
                <button type="submit" title="Save" class="button">
                    <span>
                        <span><?php echo $this->__('Save') ?></span>
                    </span>
                </button>
            </div>
        </fieldset>
    </form>
    <script type="text/javascript">
        //<![CDATA[
        var dataForm = new VarienForm('form-validate', true);
        //]]>
    </script>
<?php else: ?>
    <h2><?php echo $this->__('There was a problem loading the
registry') ?></h2>
<?php endif; ?>
```

Let's continue by adding the block and templates for the edit action:

1. Open the `mdg_giftregistry.xml` layout file.

2. Add the following code inside the `<mdg_gifregistry_index_edit>` node (the file location is `app/design/frontend/base/default/layout/mdg_giftregistry.xml`):

```
<reference name="content">
    <block name="giftregistry.edit" type="core/template"
    template="mdg/edit.phtml" as="giftregistry_edit"/>
</reference>
```

Once that is set, we can try creating a couple of test registries and modifying their properties.

Here's a challenge for you. As with the controller, the edit and new form can be combined into a single reusable form. Try to combine them to see the answer with the complete code and full breakdown, visit http://www.magedevguide.com/challenge/chapter4/4.

SearchController blocks and views

For our search controller, we will need a search template for our index. For the results, we can actually reuse the registry list template by simply making a change to our controller by following these steps:

1. Navigate to the template folder.

2. Create a file called search.phtml.

3. Add the following code (the file location is app/design/frontend/base/ default/template/mdg/search.phtml):

```php
<?php $helper = Mage::helper('mdg_giftregistry'); ?>
<form action="<?php echo $this->getUrl('giftregistry/search/
results/') ?>" method="post" id="form-validate">
    <fieldset>
        <?php echo $this->getBlockHtml('formkey')?>
        <ul class="form-list">
            <li>
                <label for="type">Event type</label>
                <select name="type" id="type">
                    <?php foreach($helper->getEventTypes() as
$type): ?>
                        <option id="<?php echo $type->getTypeId();
?>" value="<?php echo $type->getCode(); ?>">
                            <?php echo $type->getName(); ?>
                        </option>
                    <?php endforeach; ?>
                </select>
            </li>
            <li class="field">
                <label class="giftreg" for="name"><?php echo
$this->__('Event Name') ?></label>
                <input type="text" name="name" id="name" value=""
title="Event Name"/>
            </li>
            <li class="field">
                <label class="giftreg" for="location"><?php echo
$this->__('Event Location') ?></label>
```

```
                <input type="text" name="location" id="location"
value="" title="Event Location"/>
            </li>
            <li class="field">
                <label class="giftreg" for="country"><?php echo
$this->__('Event Country') ?></label>
                <input type="text" name="country" id="country"
value="" title="Event Country"/>
            </li>
        </ul>
        <div class="buttons-set">
            <button type="submit" title="Save" class="button">
                <span>
                    <span><?php echo $this->__('Save') ?></
span>
                </span>
            </button>
        </div>
    </fieldset>
</form>
<script type="text/javascript">
    //<![CDATA[
    var dataForm = new VarienForm('form-validate', true);
    //]]>
</script>
```

A couple of things to notice:

- We are using the helper model to populate the `Event` type IDs
- We are posting directly to the search/results

Now, let's make the appropriate change to our layout file:

1. Open `mdg_giftregistry.xml`.
2. Add the following code inside `<mdg_gifregistry_search_index>` (the file location is `app/design/frontend/base/default/layout/mdg_giftregistry.xml`):

```
<reference name="content">
    <block name="giftregistry.search" type="core/template"
template="mdg/search.phtml" as="giftregistry_search"/>
</reference>
```

For the search results, we don't need to create a new block type since we are passing the results collection directly to the block. In the layout, our changes will be minimal, and we can reuse the list block for displaying the search registry results.

However, we do need to make a change in the controller. We need to change the function from `setResults()` to `setCustomerRegistries()`.

The file location is `app/code/local/Mdg/Giftregistry/controllers/SearchController.php`. Refer to the following code:

```
public function resultsAction()
{
    $this->loadLayout();
    if ($searchParams = $this->getRequest()->getParam('search_
params')) {
        $results = Mage::getModel('mdg_giftregistry/entity')-
>getCollection();
        if($searchParams['type']){
            $results->addFieldToFilter('type_id',
$searchParams['type']);
        }
        if($searchParams['date']){
            $results->addFieldToFilter('event_date',
$searchParams['date']);
        }
        if($searchParams['location']){
            $results->addFieldToFilter('event_location',
$searchParams['location']);
        }
        $this->getLayout()->getBlock('mdg_giftregistry.search.
results')
            ->setCustomerRegistries($results);
    }
    $this->renderLayout();
    return $this;
}
```

Finally, let's update the layout files by following these steps:

1. Open `mdg_giftregistry.xml`.

2. Add the following code inside `<mdg_gifregistry_search_results>` (the file location is `app/design/frontend/base/default/layout/mdg_giftregistry.xml`):

```
<reference name="content">
    <block name="giftregistry.results" type="mdg_giftregistry/
list" template="mdg/list.phtml"/>
</reference>
```

And that would be the end of our `SearchController` template; however, there is a problem that our search results are displaying. For the delete and edit links of a registry, we need a way to restrict these links only to the owner.

We can do that with the following `Helper` function:

The file location is `app/code/local/Mdg/Giftregistry/Helper/Data.php`. Refer to the following code:

```php
public function isRegistryOwner($registryCustomerId)
{
    $currentCustomer = Mage::getSingleton('customer/session')-
>getCustomer();
    if($currentCustomer && $currentCustomer->getId() ==
$registryCustomerId)
    {
        return true;
    }
    return false;
}
```

And let's update our template to use the new `helper` method.

The file location is `app/design/frontend/base/default/template/mdg/list.phtml`. Refer to the following code:

```php
<?php
    $_collection = $this->getCustomerRegistries();
    $helper = Mage::helper('mdg_giftregistry')
?>
<div class="customer-list">
    <?php if (!$_collection->count()): ?>
        <h2><?php echo $this->__('You have no registries.') ?></h2>
        <a href="<?php echo $this->getUrl('giftregistry/index/new')
?>">
            <?php echo $this->__('Click Here to create a new Gift
Registry') ?>
        </a>
    <?php else: ?>
        <ul>
            <?php foreach($_collection as $registry): ?>
                <li>
                    <h3><?php echo $registry->getEventName(); ?></h3>
                    <p><strong><?php echo $this->__('Event Date:') ?>
<?php echo $registry->getEventDate(); ?></strong></p>
```

```
                <p><strong><?php echo $this->__('Event Location:')
?> <?php echo $registry->getEventLocation(); ?></strong></p>
                <a href="<?php echo $this->getUrl('giftregistry/
view/view', array('_query' => array('registry_id' => $registry-
>getEntityId())))) ?>">
                    <?php echo $this->__('View Registry') ?>
                </a>
                <?php if($helper->isRegistryOwner($registry-
>getCustomerId())): ?>
                    <a href="<?php echo $this-
>getUrl('giftregistry/index/edit', array('_query' => array('registry_
id' => $registry->getEntityId())))) ?>">
                        <?php echo $this->__('Edit Registry') ?>
                    </a>
                    <a href="<?php echo $this-
>getUrl('giftregistry/index/delete', array('_query' =>
array('registry_id' => $registry->getEntityId())))) ?>">
                        <?php echo $this->__('Delete Registry') ?>
                    </a>
                <?php endif; ?>

            </li>
        <?php endforeach; ?>
    </ul>
    <?php endif; ?>
</div>
```

ViewController block and views

For our view, we just need to create a new template file and a new entry in the `layout.xml` file:

1. Navigate to the template directory.
2. Create a template called `view.phtml`.
3. Add the following code (the file location is `app/design/frontend/base/default/template/mdg/view.phtml`):

```
<?php $registry = Mage::registry('loaded_registry'); ?>
<h3><?php echo $registry->getEventName(); ?></h3>
<p><strong><?php $this->__('Event Date:') ?> <?php echo $registry-
>getEventDate(); ?></strong></p>
<p><strong><?php $this->__('Event Location:') ?> <?php echo
$registry->getEventLocation(); ?></strong></p>
```

4. Update the layout XML file, `<mdg_gifregistry_view_view>`.

```
<reference name="content">
    <block name="giftregistry.view" type="core/template"
template="mdg/view.phtml" as="giftregistry_view"/>
</reference>
```

 Here's a challenge for you. Improve the view form to return an error if there is not an actual loaded registry. To see the answer with the complete code and full breakdown, visit `http://www.magedevguide.com/challenge/chapter4/5.`

Adding products to the registry

We are almost at the end of the chapter, and we are yet to cover how to add products to our registries. Due to space concerns in this book, I decided to move this section to `http://www.magedevguide.com/chapter6/adding-products-registry.`

Summary

In this chapter, we have covered a lot of ground. We have learned how to extend the frontend of Magento and how to work with routes and controllers.

The Magento layout system allows us to modify and control blocks and display it on our store. We also started working with Magento Data models, and we learned how to use them, as well as how to handle and manipulate our data.

We have only touched the surface of the frontend development and of the Data models. In the next chapter, we will expand a little bit more on the topics of configuration, models, and data, and we will explore and create an admin section on the Magento backend.

5

Backend Development

In the previous chapter, we added all the frontend functionality for the gift registry. Now customers are able to create registries and add products to the customer registries, and in general have full control over their own registries.

In this chapter, we are going to build all the functionalities that store owners need to manage and control the registries through the backend of Magento.

Magento backend can be considered in many senses a separate application from the frontend of Magento; it uses a completely separate theme, style, and a different base controller.

For our gift registry, we want to allow store owners to see all customer registries, modify the information, and add and remove items. In this chapter, we will cover the following:

- Extending the Adminhtml with configuration
- Using the grid widget
- Using the form widget
- Restricting access and permissions with Access Control Lists

Extending the Adminhtml

`Mage_Adminhtml` is a single module that provides all the backend functionalities for Magento through the usage of configuration. As we learned before, Magento uses scopes for defining the configuration. In the previous chapter, we used the frontend scope to set up the configuration for our custom module.

To modify the backend, we need to create a new scope in our configuration file called `admin`. Perform the following steps to do so:

1. Open the `config.xml` file, which can be found at the location `app/code/loca/Mdg/Giftregistry/etc/`.

2. Add the following code to it:

```
<admin>
 <routers>
   <giftregistry>
     <use>admin</use>
       <args>
           <module>Mdg_Giftregistry_Adminhmtl</module>
           <frontName>giftregistry</frontName>
       </args>
   </giftregistry>
 </routers>
</admin>
```

This code is very similar to the one we used before to specify our frontend route; however, by declaring the route this way we are breaking an unwritten Magento design pattern.

In order to keep things consistent on the backend, all new modules should extend the main admin route.

Instead of defining the route with the previous code, we are creating a completely new admin route. Normally, you don't want to do this for the Magento backend unless you are creating a new route that requires admin access but not the rest of the Magento backend. A callback URL for an admin action would be a good example of something like this.

Fortunately, there is a very easy way to share route names among Magento modules.

Sharing route names was introduced in Magento 1.3 but to this day, we still see extensions that don't use this pattern properly.

Let's update our code:

1. Open the `config.xml` file, which can be found at the location `app/code/loca/Mdg/Giftregistry/etc/`.

2. Update the routes configuration with the following code:

```
<admin>
 <routers>
   <adminhtml>
     <args>
       <modules>
          <mdg_giftregistry before="Mage_Adminhtml">Mdg_
Giftregistry_Adminhtml</mdg_giftregistry>
       </modules>
     </args>
   </adminhtml>
 </routers>
</admin>
```

After making this change, we can properly access our admin controllers through the admin namespace; for example, `http://magento.localhost.com/giftregistry/index` would now be `http://magento.localhost.com/admin/giftregistry/index`.

Our next step will be to create a new controller that we can use to manage the customer registries. We will call this controller `GiftregistryController.php`. Perform the following steps to do so:

1. Navigate to your module controllers folder.

2. Create a new folder called `Adminhtml`.

3. Create the file called `GiftregistryController.php` at the location `app/code/loca/Mdg/Giftregistry/controllers/Adminhtml/`.

4. Add the following code to it:

```php
<?php
class Mdg_Giftregistry_Adminhtml_GiftregistryController extends
Mage_Adminhtml_Controller_Action
{
    public function indexAction()
    {
        $this->loadLayout();
        $this->renderLayout();
        return $this;
```

```
        }

        public function editAction()
        {
            $this->loadLayout();
            $this->renderLayout();
            return $this;
        }

        public function saveAction()
        {
            $this->loadLayout();
            $this->renderLayout();
            return $this;
        }

        public function newAction()
        {
            $this->loadLayout();
            $this->renderLayout();
            return $this;
        }

        public function massDeleteAction()
        {
            $this->loadLayout();
            $this->renderLayout();
            return $this;
        }
    }
```

Notice something important: this new controller extends `Mage_Adminhtml_Controller_Action` instead of `Mage_Core_Controller_Front_Action`, which we had been using so far. The reason for this is that the `Adminhtml` controller has additional validation to prevent non-admin users to access their actions.

Notice that we are placing our controller inside a new subfolder inside the `controllers/` directory; by using this subdirectory, we are keeping the frontend and backend controllers organized. This is a widely accepted Magento standard practice.

For now, let's leave this blank controller alone, and let's extend the Magento backend navigation and add some extra tabs to the customer edit page.

Back to the configuration

As we have seen so far, most of the time Magento is controlled by XML configuration files and the backend layout is no different. We need to create a new `adminhtml` layout file. Perform the following steps to do so:

1. Navigate to the design folder.

2. Create a new folder called `adminhtml` and inside it create the following folder structure:

   - `adminhtml/`
   - `--default/`
   - `----default/`
   - `------template/`
   - `------layout/`

3. Inside the `layout` folder let's create a new layout file called `giftregistry.xml` at the location `app/code/design/adminhtml/default/default/layout/`.

4. Copy the following code into the layout file:

```xml
<?xml version="1.0"?>
<layout version="0.1.0">
    <adminhtml_customer_edit>
        <reference name="left">
            <reference name="customer_edit_tabs">
                <block type="mdg_giftregistry/adminhtml_customer_
edit_tab_giftregistry" name="tab_giftregistry_main" template="mdg_
giftregistry/giftregistry/customer/main.phtml">
                </block>
                <action method="addTab">
                 <name>mdg_giftregistry</name>
                <block>tab_giftregistry_main</block>
            </action>
            </reference>
        </reference>
    </adminhtml_customer_edit>
</layout>
```

We also need to add the new layout file into the `config.xml` module. Perform the following steps to do so:

1. Navigate to the `etc/` folder.

2. Open the `config.xml` file, which can be found at the location `app/code/loca/Mdg/Giftregistry/etc/`.

3. Copy the following code into the `config.xml` file:

```
...
<adminhtml>
    <layout>
        <updates>
            <mdg_giftregistry
            module="mdg_giftregistry">
                <file>giftregistry.xml</file>
            </mdg_giftregistry>
        </updates>
    </layout>
</adminhtml>
...
```

What we are doing inside the layout is creating a new container block and declaring a new tab that contains this block.

Let's quickly test our changes so far by logging in to the Magento backend and opening a customer information by going into **Customer Manager** located at **Customers | Manage Customers**.

We should get the following error in the backend:

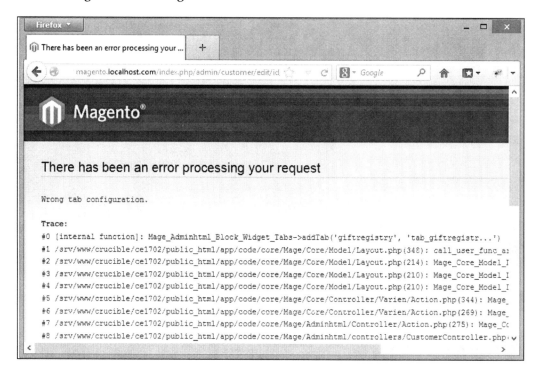

This is because we are trying to add a block that has not been declared yet; to fix this, we need to create a new block class. Perform the following steps to do so:

1. Navigate to the blocks folder and create a new block class following the directory structure called `Giftregistry.php` at the location `app/code/loca/Mdg/Giftregistry/Block/Adminhtml/Customer/Edit/Tab/`.

2. Add the following code to it:

```php
<?php
class Mdg_Giftregistry_Block_Adminhtml_Customer_Edit_Tab_
Giftregistry
    extends Mage_Adminhtml_Block_Template
    implements Mage_Adminhtml_Block_Widget_Tab_Interface {

    public function __construct()
    {
        $this->setTemplate
        ('mdg/giftregistry/customer/main.phtml');
        parent::_construct();
    }

    public function getCustomerId()
    {
        return Mage::registry('current_customer')->getId();
    }

    public function getTabLabel()
    {
        return $this->__('GiftRegistry List');
    }

    public function getTabTitle()
    {
        return $this->__
        ('Click to view the customer Gift Registries');
    }

    public function canShowTab()
    {
        return true;
    }

    public function isHidden()
    {
        return false;
    }
}
```

There are a couple of interesting things happening with this block class. For starters, we are extending a different block class, `Mage_Adminhtml_Block_Template`, and implementing a new interface, `Mage_Adminhtml_Block_Widget_Tab_Interface`. This is done in order to access all the features and functionalities of the Magento backend.

We are also setting the block template inside the construct function of our class; also under the `getCustomerId`, we are making use of the Magento global variables to get the current customer.

Our next step will be to create the corresponding template file for this block, otherwise we would get an error on the block initialization.

1. Create a template file called `main.phtml` at the location `app/code/design/adminhtml/default/default/template/mdg/giftregistry/customer/`.

2. Copy the following code into it:

```
<div class="entry-edit">
    <div class="entry-edit-head">
        <h4 class="icon-head head-customer-view"><?php echo
        $this->__('Customer Gift Registry List') ?></h4>
    </div>
    <table cellspacing="2" class="box-left">
        <tr>
            <td>
                Nothing here
            </td>
        </tr>
    </table>
</div>
```

For now, we are just adding placeholder content to the template so that we can actually see our tabs in action; now, if we go to the customer section in the backend, we should see that a new tab is available, and clicking on that tab will display our placeholder content.

By now, we have modified the backend and added a **Customers** tab to the customer section just by changing a configuration and adding some simple blocks and a template file. But so far, this hasn't been particularly useful, so we need a way of displaying all the customer gift registries under the **Gift registry** tab.

The grid widget

Instead of having to write our own grid blocks from scratch, we can reuse the ones that have been already provided by the Magento `Adminhtml` module.

The block that we will be extending is called grid widget; the grid widget is a special type of block designed to render a collection of Magento objects in a particular table grid.

A grid widget is normally rendered inside a Grid container; the combination of both elements allow not only to display our data in a grid form but also adds search, filtering, sorting, and mass action capabilities. Perform the following steps:

1. Navigate to the block `Adminhtml/` folder and create a folder called `Giftregistry/` at the location `app/code/loca/Mdg/Giftregistry/Block/Adminhtml/Customer/Edit/Tab/`.

2. Create a class called `List.php` inside that folder.

3. Copy the following code into the `Giftregistry/List.php` file:

```php
<?php
class Mdg_Giftregistry_Block_Adminhtml_Customer_Edit_Tab_
Giftregistry_List extends Mage_Adminhtml_Block_Widget_Grid
{
    public function __construct()
    {
        parent::__construct();
        $this->setId('registryList');
        $this->setUseAjax(true);
        $this->setDefaultSort('event_date');
        $this->setFilterVisibility(false);
        $this->setPagerVisibility(false);
    }

    protected function _prepareCollection()
    {
        $collection = Mage::getModel
        ('mdg_giftregistry/entity')
            ->getCollection()
            ->addFieldToFilter('main_table.customer_id',
            $this->getRequest()->getParam('id'));
        $this->setCollection($collection);
```

```
            return parent::_prepareCollection();
        }

        protected function _prepareColumns()
        {
            $this->addColumn('entity_id', array(
                'header'   => Mage::helper
                ('mdg_giftregistry')->__('Id'),
                'width'    => 50,
                'index'    => 'entity_id',
                'sortable' => false,
            ));

            $this->addColumn('event_location', array(
                'header'   => Mage::helper
                ('mdg_giftregistry')->__('Location'),
                'index'    => 'event_location',
                'sortable' => false,
            ));

            $this->addColumn('event_date', array(
                'header'   => Mage::helper
                ('mdg_giftregistry')->__('Event Date'),
                'index'    => 'event_date',
                'sortable' => false,
            ));

            $this->addColumn('type_id', array(
                'header'   => Mage::helper
                ('mdg_giftregistry')->__('Event Type'),
                'index'    => 'type_id',
                'sortable' => false,
            ));
            return parent::_prepareColumns();
        }
    }
```

Looking at the class we just created, there are only three functions involved:

- `__construct()`
- `_prepareCollection()`
- `_prepareColumns()`

On the `__construct` function, we are specifying a few important options about our grid class. We are setting the `gridId`; the default sort to be by `eventDate`, and we are enabling pagination and filtering.

The `__prepareCollection()` function loads a collection of registries filtered by current `customerId`. This function can be used to do more complex operations in our collection too; for example, joining a secondary table to get more information about the customer or another related record.

Finally, by using the `__prepareColumns()` function, we are telling Magento which columns and attributes for our data collection should be shown and how we can render them.

Now that we have created a functional grid block, we would need to do some changes to our layout XML file in order to display it. Perform the following steps:

1. Open the `giftregistry.xml` file, which can be found at the location `app/design/adminhtml/default/default/layout/`.

2. Make the following changes:

```xml
<?xml version="1.0"?>
<layout version="0.1.0">
    <adminhtml_customer_edit>
        <reference name="left">
            <reference name="customer_edit_tabs">
                <block type="mdg_giftregistry/
                adminhtml_customer_edit_tab_giftregistry"
                name="tab_giftregistry_main"
                template="mdg/giftregistry/
                customer/main.phtml">
                    <block type="mdg_giftregistry/
                    adminhtml_customer_edit_tab_
                    giftregistry_list"
                    name="tab_giftregistry_list"
                    as="giftregistry_list" />
                </block>
                <action method="addTab">
                    <name>mdg_giftregistry</name>
                    <block>mdg_giftregistry/adminhtml_customer_
edit_tab_giftregistry</block>
                </action>
            </reference>
        </reference>
    </adminhtml_customer_edit>
</layout>
```

What we did was to add the grid block as part of our main block, but if we go to the customer edit page and click on the **Gift registry** tab, we are still seeing the old placeholder text and the grid is not displaying.

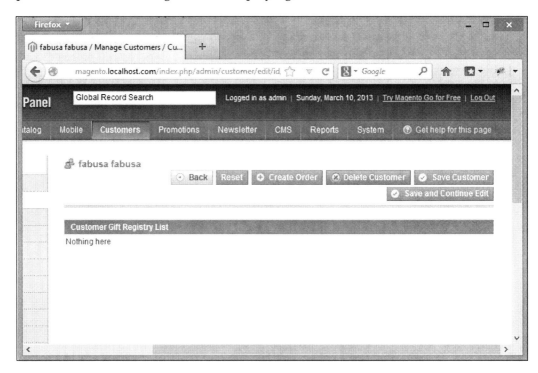

This is because we haven't made the necessary changes to our `main.phtml` template file. In order to display children blocks, we specifically need to tell the templating system to load any or a specific child; for now, we will just load our specific grid block. Perform the following steps:

1. Open the `main.phtml` template file, which can be found at the location `app/design/adminhtml/default/default/template/customer/`.

2. Replace the template code with the following:

```
<div class="entry-edit">
    <div class="entry-edit-head">
        <h4 class="icon-head head-customer-view">
        <?php echo $this->__
        ('Customer Gift Registry List') ?></h4>
    </div>
    <?php echo $this->getChildHtml('tab_giftregistry_list'); ?>
</div>
```

The `getChildHtml()` function is responsible for rendering all the child blocks.

The function `getChildHtml()` can be called with a specific child block name or without parameters; when called without parameters, it will load all the available children blocks.

In the case of our extension, we are only interested in instantiating a particular child block, so we will be passing the block name as the function parameter. Now, if we refresh the page, we should see our grid block loaded with all the gift registries available for that particular customer.

Managing the registries

Now, this is handy if we want to manage the registries for a specific customer, but it does not really help us if we want to manage all the registries available in a store. For that, we need to create a grid that loads all the available gift registries.

Since we already created a gift registry controller for the backend, we can use the index action to display all the available registries.

The first thing we need to do is to modify the Magento backend navigation to show a link to our new controller index action. Again, we can achieve this by using XML. In this particular case, we are going to create a new XML file called `adminhtml.xml`. Perform the following steps:

1. Navigate to your module `etc` folder, which can be found at the location `app/code/local/Mdg/Giftregistry/`.

2. Create a new file called `adminhtml.xml`.

3. Place the following code in that file:

```xml
<?xml version="1.0"?>
<config>
    <menu>
        <mdg_giftregistry module="mdg_giftregistry">
            <title>Gift Registry</title>
            <sort_order>71</sort_order>
            <children>
                <items module="mdg_giftregistry">
                    <title>Manage Registries</title>
                    <sort_order>0</sort_order>
                    <action>adminhtml/giftregistry/index</action>
                </items>
            </children>
        </mdg_giftregistry>
    </menu>
</config>
```

While the standard is to have this configuration added inside `adminhtml.xml`, you will likely encounter extensions where this standard is not followed. This configuration can be located inside `config.xml`.

This configuration code is creating a new main-level menu and a new child-level option under it; we are also specifying which action the menu should be mapped to, in this case, the index action of our gift registry controller.

If we refresh the backend now, we should see a new **Gift registry** menu added to the top-level navigation.

Permissions and the ACL

Sometimes we need to restrict access to certain features of our module or even the whole module based on the admin rule. Magento allows us to do this by using a power feature called **ACL** or **Access Control List**. Each role in the Magento backend can have different permissions and different ACLs.

The first step of enabling ACLs with our custom module is to define which resources should be restricted by the ACL; not so surprisingly, this is controlled by the configuration XML files. Perform the following steps:

1. Open the `adminhtml.xml` configuration file, which can be found at the location `app/code/local/Mdg/Giftregistry/etc/`.

2. Add the following code after the menu path:

```
<acl>
    <resources>
        <admin>
            <children>
                <giftregistry translate="title"
                module="mdg_giftregistry">
                    <title>Gift Registry</title>
                    <sort_order>300</sort_order>
                    <children>
                        <items translate="title"
                        module="mdg_giftregistry">
                            <title>Manage Registries</title>
                            <sort_order>0</sort_order>
                        </items>
                    </children>
                </giftregistry>
            </children>
```

```
        </admin>
      </resources>
    </acl>
```

Now, in the Magento backend, if we navigate to **System | Permissions | Roles**, select the **Administrators** role, and try to set **Roles Resources** at the bottom of the list; we can see the new ACL resources we created, as shown in the following screenshot:

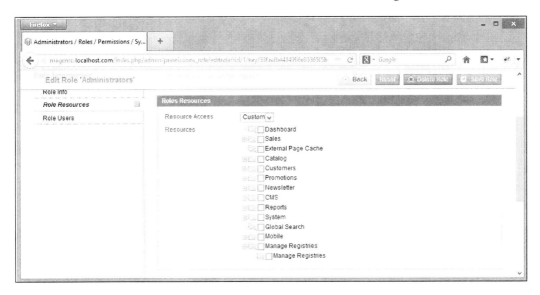

By doing this, we gain granular control over which operations each user has access to.

If we click on the **Manage Registries** menu, we should get a blank page; since we haven't created the corresponding grid block, layouts, and templates, we should see a completely blank page.

So let's start by creating the blocks that we will need for our new grid; the way we will create our gift registry grid will be slightly different from what we did for our **Customers** tab.

We need to create a grid container block and a grid block. The grid container is used to hold the grid header, the buttons, and the grid content, while the grid block is only in charge of rendering the grid with pagination, filtering, and mass actions. Perform the following steps:

1. Navigate to your block `Adminhtml` folder.

2. Create a new block called `Registries.php` at the location `app/code/local/ Mdg/Giftregistry/Block/Adminhtml/`:

3. Add the following code to it:

```php
<?php
class Mdg_Giftregistry_Block_Adminhtml_Registries extends Mage_
Adminhtml_Block_Widget_Grid_Container
{
public function __construct(){
    $this->_controller = 'adminhtml_registries';
    $this->_blockGroup = 'mdg_giftregistry';
    $this->_headerText = Mage::helper
    ('mdg_giftregistry')->__('Gift Registry Manager');
    parent::__construct();
  }
}
```

One important thing we are setting up in the `construct` function inside our grid container is the usage of protected values of `_controller` and `_blockGroup` by the Magento grid container to identify the corresponding grid block.

It is important to clarify that `$this->_controller` is not the actual controller name but the block class name and `$this->_blockGroup` is actually the module name.

Let's continue with creating the grid block, which as we learned previously has three main functions: `_construct`, `_prepareCollection()`, and `_prepareColumns()`. But in this case, we will add a new function called `_prepareMassActions()`, which allows us to modify selected sets of records without having to edit each individually. Perform the following steps:

1. Navigate to your block `Adminhtml` folder and create a new folder called `Registries`.

2. Under the `Model` folder create a new block called `Grid.php` at the location `app/code/local/Mdg/Giftregistry/Block/Adminhtml/Registries/`.

3. Add the following code to `Grid.php`:

```php
File Location: Grid.php
<?php
class Mdg_Giftregistry_Block_Adminhtml_Registries_Grid extends
Mage_Adminhtml_Block_Widget_Grid
{
    public function __construct(){
        parent::__construct();
        $this->setId('registriesGrid');
        $this->setDefaultSort('event_date');
        $this->setDefaultDir('ASC');
        $this->setSaveParametersInSession(true);
```

```
    }

    protected function _prepareCollection(){
        $collection = Mage::getModel
        ('mdg_giftregistry/entity')->getCollection();
        $this->setCollection($collection);
        return parent::_prepareCollection();
    }

    protected function _prepareColumns()
    {
        $this->addColumn('entity_id', array(
            'header'   => Mage::helper
            ('mdg_giftregistry')->__('Id'),
            'width'    => 50,
            'index'    => 'entity_id',
            'sortable' => false,
        ));

        $this->addColumn('event_location', array(
            'header'   => Mage::helper
            ('mdg_giftregistry')->__('Location'),
            'index'    => 'event_location',
            'sortable' => false,
        ));

        $this->addColumn('event_date', array(
            'header'   => Mage::helper
            ('mdg_giftregistry')->__('Event Date'),
            'index'    => 'event_date',
            'sortable' => false,
        ));

        $this->addColumn('type_id', array(
            'header'   => Mage::helper
            ('mdg_giftregistry')->__('Event Type'),
            'index'    => 'type_id',
            'sortable' => false,
        ));
        return parent::_prepareColumns();
    }

    protected function _prepareMassaction(){
    }
}
```

Backend Development

This grid code is very similar to what we had created before for the **Customers** tab, with the exception that this time we are not specifically filtering by a customer record, and we are also creating a grid container block instead of implementing a custom block.

Finally, in order to show the grid in our controller action we need to perform the following steps:

1. Open the `giftregistry.xml` file, which can be found at the location `app/code/design/adminhtml/default/default/layout/`.

2. Add the following code to it:

```
...
    <adminhtml_giftregistry_index>
        <reference name="content">
            <block type="mdg_giftregistry/adminhtml_registries"
name="registries" />
        </reference>
    </adminhtml_giftregistry_index>
...
```

Since we are using a grid container, we only need to specify the grid container block, and Magento will take care of loading the matching grid container.

There is no need to specify or create a template file for the grid or the grid container as both blocks automatically load the base templates from the `adminhtml/base/default` theme.

Now, we can check our newly added gift registry by navigating to **Gift Registry | Manage Registries** in the backend.

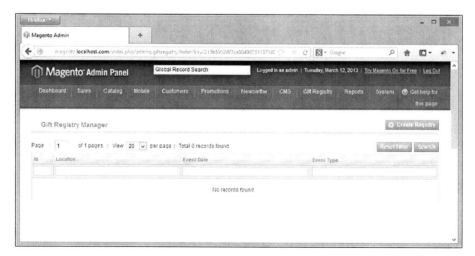

Updating in bulk with Massactions

When creating our base grid block, we defined a function called
`_prepareMassactions()`, which provides an easy way of manipulating
multiple records from the grid. In our case, for now, let's just implement
a mass delete action. Perform the following steps to do so:

1. Open the registry grid block `Grid.php`, which can be found at `app/code/`
    `local/Mdg/Giftregistry/Block/Adminhtml/Registries/`.

2. Replace the `_prepareMassaction()` function with the following code:

```
protected function _prepareMassaction(){
    $this->setMassactionIdField('entity_id');
    $this->getMassactionBlock()->
    setFormFieldName('registries');

    $this->getMassactionBlock()->addItem('delete', array(
        'label'     => Mage::helper
        ('mdg_giftregistry')->__('Delete'),
        'url'       => $this->getUrl('*/*/massDelete'),
        'confirm'   => Mage::helper
        ('mdg_giftregistry')->__('Are you sure?')
    ));
    return $this;
}
```

The way mass actions work is by passing a series of selected IDs to our specified
controller action; in this case, the `massDelete()` action will add code to iterate
through the registry collection and delete each of the specified registries. Perform
the following steps:

1. Open the `GiftregistryController.php` file, which can be found at the
    location `app/code/local/Mdg/Giftregistry/controllers/Adminhtml/`.

2. Replace the blank `massDelete()` action with the following code:

```
...
public function massDeleteAction()
{
    $registryIds = $this->
    getRequest()->getParam('registries');
        if(!is_array($registryIds)) {
            Mage::getSingleton('adminhtml/session')->
            addError(Mage::helper('mdg_giftregistry')->
            __('Please select one or more registries.'));
        } else {
            try {
```

```
$registry = Mage::getModel
('mdg_giftregistry/entity');
foreach ($registryIds as $registryId) {
    $registry->reset()
        ->load($registryId)
        ->delete();
}
Mage::getSingleton
('adminhtml/session')->addSuccess(
Mage::helper('adminhtml')->__
('Total of %d record(s) were deleted.',
count($registryIds))
);
} catch (Exception $e) {
    Mage::getSingleton
    ('adminhtml/session')->
    addError($e->getMessage());
}
}
$this->_redirect('*/*/index');
}
```

Challenge: Add two new mass actions to change the status of the registries to enable or disable respectively. To see the answer with the complete code and full breakdown, visit http://www.magedevguide.com/.

Finally, we also want to be able to edit the records listed in our grid. For that, we need to add a new function to our registries grid class; this function is called getRowUrl(), and it is used to specify the action to be taken when clicking on a grid row; in our particular case, we want to map that function to the editAction(). Perform the following steps:

1. Open the Grid.php file, which can be found at the location app/code/ local/Mdg/Giftregistry/Block/Adminhtml/Registries/.

2. Add the following function to it:

```
...
public function getRowUrl($row)
{
    return $this->getUrl('*/*/edit', array
    ('id' => $row->getEntityId()));
}
...
```

The form widget

So far, we have been working with the gift registry grid, but right now we aren't able to do much more than just getting the list of all the available registries or deleting registries in bulk. We need a way of getting the details of a specific registry; we can map this to the edit controller action.

The edit action will display the registry-specific details and will also allow us to modify the details and status of a registry. We will need to create a few blocks and templates for this action.

In order to view and edit the registry information, we need to implement a form widget block. Form widgets work in a similar fashion as the grid widget blocks and need to have a form block and a form container block that extends the Mage_Adminhtml_Block_Widget_Form_Container class. In order to create the form container, let's perform the following steps:

1. Navigate to the Registries folder.

2. Create a new class file called Edit.php at the location app/code/local/Mdg/Giftregistry/Block/Adminhtml/Registries/.

3. Add the following code to the class file:

```
class Mdg_Giftregistry_Block_Adminhtml_Registries_Edit extends
Mage_Adminhtml_Block_Widget_Form_Container
{
    public function __construct(){
        parent::__construct();
        $this->_objectId = 'id';
        $this->_blockGroup = 'registries';
        $this->_controller = 'adminhtml_giftregistry';
        $this->_mode = 'edit';

        $this->_updateButton('save', 'label', Mage::helper
        ('mdg_giftregistry')->__('Save Registry'));
        $this->_updateButton('delete', 'label',
        Mage::helper('mdg_giftregistry')->
        __('Delete Registry'));
    }

    public function getHeaderText(){
        if(Mage::registry('registries_data') &&
        Mage::registry('registries_data')->getId())
            return Mage::helper('mdg_giftregistry')->__
            ("Edit Registry '%s'", $this->
            htmlEscape(Mage::registry
            ('registries_data')->getTitle()));
```

```
                    return Mage::helper('mdg_giftregistry')->__
                    ('Add Registry');
          }
      }
```

Similar to the grid widget, the form container widget will automatically identify and load the matching form block.

One additional protected attribute that is being declared in the form container is the mode attribute; this protected attribute is used by the container to specify the location of the form block.

We can find the code responsible for creating the form block inside the `Mage_Adminhtml_Block_Widget_Form_Container` class:

```
$this->getLayout()->createBlock($this->_blockGroup . '/' . $this->_
controller . '_' . $this->_mode . '_form')
```

Now that we have created the form container block, we can proceed to create the matching form block. Perform the following steps to do so:

1. Navigate to the `Registries` folder.

2. Create a new folder called `Edit`.

3. Create a new file called `Form.php` at the location `app/code/local/Mdg/Giftregistry/Block/Adminhtml/Registries/Edit/`.

4. Add the following code to it:

```php
<?php
class Mdg_Giftregistry_Block_Adminhtml_Registries_Edit_Form
extends  Mage_Adminhtml_Block_Widget_Form
{
    protected function _prepareForm(){
        $form = new Varien_Data_Form(array(
            'id' => 'edit_form',
            'action' => $this->getUrl('*/*/save', array
            ('id' => $this->getRequest()->getParam('id'))),
            'method' => 'post',
            'enctype' => 'multipart/form-data'
        ));
        $form->setUseContainer(true);
        $this->setForm($form);

        if (Mage::getSingleton
        ('adminhtml/session')->getFormData()){
            $data = Mage::getSingleton
            ('adminhtml/session')->getFormData();
```

```
    Mage::getSingleton
    ('adminhtml/session')->setFormData(null);
}elseif(Mage::registry('registry_data'))
    $data = Mage::registry
    ('registry_data')->getData();

$fieldset = $form->addFieldset('registry_form',
array('legend'=>Mage::helper('mdg_giftregistry')
->__('Gift Registry information')));

$fieldset->addField('type_id', 'text', array(
    'label'    => Mage::helper
    ('mdg_giftregistry')->__('Registry Id'),
    'class'    => 'required-entry',
    'required' => true,
    'name'     => 'type_id',
));

$fieldset->addField('website_id', 'text', array(
    'label'    => Mage::helper
    ('mdg_giftregistry')->__('Website Id'),
    'class'    => 'required-entry',
    'required' => true,
    'name'     => 'website_id',
));

$fieldset->addField
('event_location', 'text', array(
    'label'    => Mage::helper
    ('mdg_giftregistry')->__('Event Location'),
    'class'    => 'required-entry',
    'required' => true,
    'name'     => 'event_location',
));

$fieldset->addField('event_date', 'text', array(
    'label'    => Mage::helper
    ('mdg_giftregistry')->__('Event Date'),
    'class'    => 'required-entry',
    'required' => true,
    'name'     => 'event_date',
));

$fieldset->addField('event_country', 'text', array(
    'label'    => Mage::helper
    ('mdg_giftregistry')->__('Event Country'),
    'class'    => 'required-entry',
    'required' => true,
```

```
                    'name'        => 'event_country',
            ));

            $form->setValues($data);
            return parent::_prepareForm();
        }
    }
```

We also need to modify our layout file and tell Magento to load our form container.

Copy the following code to the layout file `giftregistry.xml`, which can be found at the location `app/code/design/adminhtml/default/default/layout/`:

```xml
<?xml version="1.0"?>
<layout version="0.1.0">
    ...
    <adminhtml_giftregistry_edit>
        <reference name="content">
            <block type="mdg_giftregistry/adminhtml_registries_edit"
name="new_registry_tabs" />
        </reference>
    </adminhtml_giftregistry_edit>
    ...
```

We can check out our progress at this point by going into the Magento backend and clicking on one of our example registries. We should see the following form:

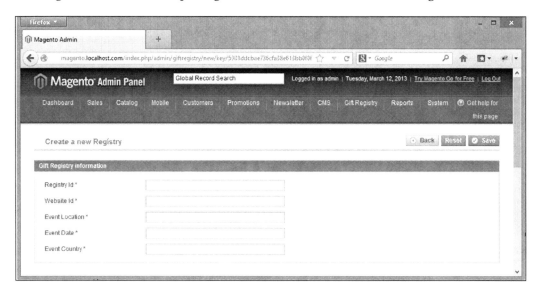

But there seems to be an issue. None of the data is loaded; we just have an empty form, so we have to modify our controller `editAction()` in order to load the data.

Loading the data

Let's start by modifying `editAction()` inside our `GiftregistryController.php`
file, which can be found at the location `app/code/local/Mdg/Giftregistry/`
`controllers/Adminhtml/`:

```
...
public function editAction()
{
    $id       = $this->getRequest()->getParam('id', null);
    $registry = Mage::getModel('mdg_giftregistry/entity');

    if ($id) {
        $registry->load((int) $id);
        if ($registry->getId()) {
            $data = Mage::getSingleton
            ('adminhtml/session')->getFormData(true);
            if ($data) {
                $registry->setData($data)->setId($id);
            }
        } else {
            Mage::getSingleton('adminhtml/session')->addError
            (Mage::helper('awesome')->__
            ('The Gift Registry does not exist'));
            $this->_redirect('*/*/');
        }
    }
    Mage::register('registry_data', $registry);

    $this->loadLayout();
    $this->getLayout()->getBlock('head')->setCanLoadExtJs(true);
    $this->renderLayout();
}
```

What we are doing inside our `editAction()` is to check for a registry with the
same ID, and if it exists, we will load that registry entity and make it available to
our form. Previously, when adding the form code to the file `app/code/local/Mdg/`
`Giftregistry/Block/Adminhtml/Registries/Edit/Form.php`, we included
the following:

```
...
if (Mage::getSingleton('adminhtml/session')->getFormData()){
    $data = Mage::getSingleton('adminhtml/session')->getFormData();
    Mage::getSingleton('adminhtml/session')->setFormData(null);
}elseif(Mage::registry('registry_data'))
    $data = Mage::registry('registry_data')->getData();
...
```

Now, we can test our changes by reloading the form:

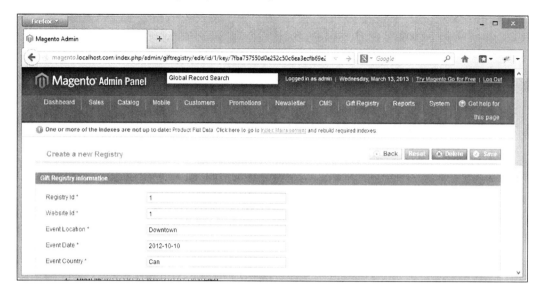

Saving the data

Now that we have created the form for editing a registry, we need to create the corresponding action to process and save the data posted by the form. We can use the save form action to handle this. Perform the following steps:

1. Open the `GiftregistryController.php` class, which can be found at the location `app/code/local/Mdg/Giftregistry/controllers/Adminhtml/`.

2. Replace the blank `saveAction()` function with the following code:

```
public function saveAction()
{
    if ($this->getRequest()->getPost())
    {
        try {
            $data = $this->getRequest()->getPost();
            $id = $this->getRequest()->getParam('id');

            if ($data && $id) {
```

```
        $registry = Mage::getModel
        ('mdg_giftregistry/entity')->load($id);
        $registry->setData($data);
        $registry->save();
          $this->_redirect('*/*/edit', array
          ('id' => $this->getRequest()
          ->getParam('registry_id')));
      }
    } catch (Exception $e) {
      $this->_getSession()->addError(
          Mage::helper('mdg_giftregistry')->__
          ('An error occurred while saving the
          registry data. Please review the log
          and try again.')
      );
      Mage::logException($e);
      $this->_redirect('*/*/edit', array
      ('id' => $this->getRequest()->
      getParam('registry_id')));
      return $this;
    }
  }
}
```

Let's break down what this code is doing step by step:

1. We check if the request has valid post data.
2. We check that both the $data and $id variables are set.
3. If both variables are set, we load a new registry entity and set the data.
4. Finally, we try to save the registry entity.

The first thing we do is to check that the data posted is not empty and that we are getting a registry ID as part of the parameters; we also check if the registry ID is a valid instance of the registry entity.

Summary

In this chapter, we learned how to modify and extend the Magento backend to our specific needs.

Whereas, the frontend extends the functionality that the customers and users can use; extending the backend allows us to control this custom functionality and how customers interact with it.

Grids and forms are important parts of the Magento backend, and by using them properly, we can add a lot of functionality without having to write a lot of code or reinvent the wheel.

Finally, we learned how to use the permissions and Magento ACL to control and restrict the permissions of our custom extension after extension, as well as Magento in general.

In the next chapter, we will dive deep into the Magento API, and we will learn how to extend it to manipulate our registry data using several methods such as SOAP, XML-RPC, and REST.

6
The Magento API

In the previous chapter, we extended the Magento backend and learned how to use some of the backend components so that store owners can manage and manipulate the gift registry data of each customer.

In this chapter we will cover the following topics:

- The Magento Core API
- The multiple API protocols available (REST, SOAP, XML-RPC)
- How to use the Core API
- How to extend the API to implement new functionality
- How to restrict parts of the API to specific web user roles

While the backend provides an interface for day-to-day operations, sometimes we will need to access and/or transmit data from and to third-party systems. Magento already provides API functionality for most of the core features, but for our custom gift registry extension, we will need to extend the `Mage_Api` functionality.

The Core API

Often while talking about the API, I heard developers talking about the Magento SOAP API or the Magento XML-RPC API or the RESTful API. But the important fact is that these are not separate APIs for each of these protocols; instead, Magento has a single Core API.

As you might notice, Magento is built mostly around abstraction and configuration (mostly XML), and the Magento API is no exception. We have a single core API and adapters for each of the different protocol types. This is incredibly flexible, and if we want to, we can implement our own adapter for another protocol.

The core Magento API gives us the ability to manage products, categories, attributes, orders, and invoices. This is done by exposing three of the core modules:

- `Mage_Catalog`
- `Mage_Sales`
- `Mage_Customer`

The API supports three different types: SOAP, XML-RPC, and REST. Now, if you have done web development outside Magento and with other APIs, it is most likely that those APIs have been RESTful APIs.

Before we jump into the specifics of the Magento API architecture, it is important that we understand the differences between each of the supported API types.

XML-RPC

XML-RPC was one of the first protocols supported by Magento and it is the oldest of them all. This protocol has a single endpoint on which all the functions are called and accessed.

 XML-RPC is a **remote procedure call** (**RPC**) protocol that uses XML to encode its calls and HTTP as a transport mechanism.

Since there is only a single endpoint, XML-RPC is easy to use and maintain; its purpose is to be a simple and effective protocol for sending and receiving data. The implementation uses straightforward XML to encode and decode a remote procedure call along with the parameters.

However, this comes at a cost, and there are several problems with the whole XML-RPC protocol:

- Lack of discoverability and documentation.

- Parameters are anonymous and XML-RPC relies on the order of the parameters to differentiate them.

- Simplicity is the greatest strength and the greatest issue with XML-RPC. While most of the tasks can easily be achieved with XML-RPC, some tasks will require you to bend over backwards to achieve something that should be straightforward to implement.

SOAP was designed to address XML-RPC limitations and provide a more robust protocol.

For more information about XML-RPC you can go to the following link:

`http://en.wikipedia.org/wiki/XML-RPC`

SOAP

The SOAP v1 was one of the first protocols supported by Magento along with XML-RPC since Magento 1.3 SOAP v2.

 SOAP, originally defined as **Simple Object Access Protocol**, is a protocol specification for exchanging structured information in the implementation of web services in computer networks.

A **SOAP request** is basically an HTTP POST request containing a SOAP envelope, a header, and a body.

The core of SOAP is **Web Services Description Language (WSDL)**, which is basically XML. WSDL is used to describe the functionality of a web service, in this case our API methods. This is achieved by using the following series of predetermined objects:

- **Types**: These are used to describe the data transmitted with the API; types are defined using XML Schema, a special language for this purpose

- **Message**: This is used to specify the information needed to perform each one of the operations; in the case of Magento, our API methods will always use request and respond messages

- **Port type**: These are used to define the operations that can be performed and their corresponding messages

- **Port**: This is used to define the connection point; in the case of Magento, a simple string is used

- **Service**: This is used to specify which functions are exposed through the API

- **Bindings**: They are used to define the operations and the interface with the SOAP protocol

 For more information about the SOAP protocol you can refer to the following website:

`http://en.wikipedia.org/wiki/SOAP`

All the WSDL configuration is contained inside each module `wsdl.xml` file; for example, let's take a look at an excerpt of the Catalog Product API:

The file location is `app/code/local/Mdg/Giftregistry/etc/wsdl.xml`.

```xml
<?xml version="1.0" encoding="UTF-8"?>
<definitions xmlns:typens="urn:{{var wsdl.name}}" xmlns:xsd="http://
www.w3.org/2001/XMLSchema"
            xmlns:soap="http://schemas.xmlsoap.org/wsdl/soap/"
            xmlns:soapenc="http://schemas.xmlsoap.org/soap/encoding/"
xmlns:wsdl="http://schemas.xmlsoap.org/wsdl/"
            xmlns="http://schemas.xmlsoap.org/wsdl/"
            name="{{var wsdl.name}}" targetNamespace="urn:{{var wsdl.
name}}">
    <types>
        <schema xmlns="http://www.w3.org/2001/XMLSchema"
targetNamespace="urn:Magento">
        ...
            <complexType name="catalogProductEntity">
                <all>
                    <element name="product_id" type="xsd:string"/>
                    <element name="sku" type="xsd:string"/>
                    <element name="name" type="xsd:string"/>
                    <element name="set" type="xsd:string"/>
                    <element name="type" type="xsd:string"/>
                    <element name="category_ids"
type="typens:ArrayOfString"/>
                    <element name="website_ids"
type="typens:ArrayOfString"/>
                </all>
            </complexType>

        </schema>
    </types>
    <message name="catalogProductListResponse">
        <part name="storeView" type="typens:catalogProductEntityArr
ay"/>
    </message>
  ...
    <portType name="{{var wsdl.handler}}PortType">
    ...
```

```
        <operation name="catalogProductList">
            <documentation>Retrieve products list by filters</
documentation>
            <input message="typens:catalogProductListRequest"/>
            <output message="typens:catalogProductListResponse"/>
        </operation>
        ...
    </portType>
    <binding name="{{var wsdl.handler}}Binding" type="typens:{{var
wsdl.handler}}PortType">
        <soap:binding style="rpc" transport="http://schemas.xmlsoap.
org/soap/http"/>
        ...
        <operation name="catalogProductList">
            <soap:operation soapAction="urn:{{var wsdl.handler}}
Action"/>
            <input>
                <soap:body namespace="urn:{{var wsdl.name}}"
use="encoded"
                            encodingStyle="http://schemas.xmlsoap.org/
soap/encoding/"/>
            </input>
            <output>
                <soap:body namespace="urn:{{var wsdl.name}}"
use="encoded"
                            encodingStyle="http://schemas.xmlsoap.org/
soap/encoding/"/>
            </output>
        </operation>
        ...
    </binding>
    <service name="{{var wsdl.name}}Service">
        <port name="{{var wsdl.handler}}Port" binding="typens:{{var
wsdl.handler}}Binding">
            <soap:address location="{{var wsdl.url}}"/>
        </port>
    </service>
</definitions>
```

By using WSDL we can document, list, and support more complex data types.

RESTful API

The RESTful API is the new addition to the family of protocols supported by Magento and is only available on Magento CE 1.7 or older.

 A **RESTful web service** (also called a **RESTful web API**) is a web service implemented using HTTP and the principles of REST.

A RESTful API can be defined by the following three aspects:

- It makes usage of the standard of HTTP methods, such as GET, POST, DELETE, and PUT
- Its exposed URIs are formatted in a directory-like structure
- It uses JSON or XML to transfer information

 The REST API supports the response in two formats, which are XML and JSON.

One of the advantages that REST has over SOAP and XML-RPC is that all interaction with the REST API is done through the HTTP protocol, meaning it can be used by any programming language virtually.

The Magento REST API has the following characteristics:

- Resources are accessed by making an HTTP request to the Magento API service
- The service replies with the data for the request or a status indicator or even both
- All resources can be accessed through `https://magento.localhost.com/api/rest/`
- Resources return HTTP status codes, such as `HTTP Status Code 200`, to indicate success on a response, or `HTTP Status Code 400` to indicate a bad request
- Request to a particular resource is done by adding a particular path to the base URL (`https://magento.localhost.com/api/rest/`)

REST uses **HTTP verbs** to manage the states of resources. In the Magento implementation four verbs are available: GET, POST, PUT, and DELETE. For this reason, using the RESTful API is trivial in most cases.

Using the API

Now that we have clarified each of the available protocols, let's explore what we can do with the Magento API and how to do it with each of the available protocols.

We will use the product endpoint as an example for accessing and working with the different API protocols.

 The examples are provided in PHP and these use three different protocols. For complete examples in PHP and to see examples in other programming languages visit http://magedevguide.com.

Setting up the API credentials for XML-RPC/SOAP

Before we get started, we need to create a set of web service credentials in order to access the API functions.

The first thing we need to set up is the API user role. **Roles** control the permissions for the API by using **Access Control Lists** (**ACL**). By implementing this design pattern, Magento is able to restrict certain parts of its API to specific users.

Later in this chapter, we will learn how we can add our custom functions to the ACL and secure our custom extensions' API methods. For now, we just need to create a role with full permissions by executing the following steps:

1. Go to the Magento backend.
2. Go to **System** | **Web Services** | **Roles** from the main navigation menu.
3. Click on the **Add New Role** button.

4. As shown in the following screenshot, you will be requested to provide a role name and specify the role resources:

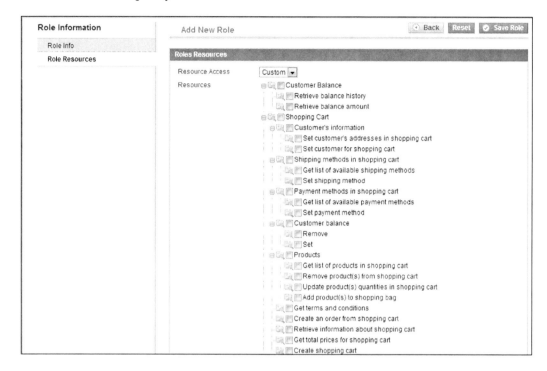

5. By default, the **Resources Access** option is set to **Custom** and no resources are selected. In our case, we will change the **Resource Access** option by selecting **All** from the drop-down menu.

6. Click on the **Save Role** button.

Now that we have a valid role in our store, let's proceed to create a web API user:

1. Go to the Magento backend.

2. Go to **System | Web Services | Users** from the main navigation menu.

3. Click on the **Add New User** button.

4. Next, we will be asked for the user information as shown in the following screenshot:

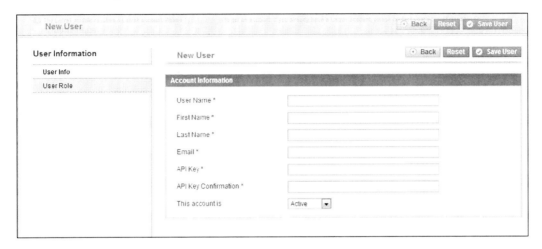

5. In the **API Key** and **API Key Confirmation** fields enter your desired password.
6. Click on the **User Role** tab.
7. Select the user role that we just created.
8. Click on the **Save User** button.

The reason that we need to create a username and role for accessing the API is that every single API function requires a session token to be passed as a parameter.

For that reason, every time we need to use the API, the first call that we have to make is to the `login` function, which will return a valid session token ID.

Setting up the REST API credentials

The new RESTful API is slightly different in terms of authentication; instead of using the traditional Magento web service users, it uses a three-legged OAuth 1.0 protocol to provide authentication.

OAuth works by asking the user to authorize its application. When the user registers an application, he/she needs to fill in the following fields:

- **User**: This is a customer, who has an account with Magento and can use the services with the API.
- **Consumer**: This is a third-party application that uses OAuth to access the Magento API.

- **Consumer Key**: This is a unique value used to identify a user with Magento.

- **Consumer Secret**: This is a secret used by the customer to guarantee the ownership of the consumer key. This value is never passed in the request.

- **Request Token**: This value is used by the consumer (application) to obtain authorization from the user to access the API resources.

- **Access Token**: This is returned in exchange of the request token and on successful authentication.

Let's proceed to register our application by going to **System | Web Services | REST - OAuth Consumers** and selecting **Add New** in the **Admin** panel:

 One important thing to notice is that a callback URL must be defined, to which the user will be redirected after successfully authorizing the application.

Our first step is to learn how to get this session token ID on each of the available API protocols.

To get session token ID in XML-RPC, we need to execute the following code:

```
$apiUser = 'username';
$apiKey = 'password';
$client = new Zend_XmlRpc_Client('http://ourhost.com/api/xmlrpc/');
// We authenticate ourselves and get a session token id
$sessionId = $client->call('login', array($apiUser, $apiKey));
```

To get a session token ID in SOAP v2, we need to execute the following code:

```
$apiUser = 'username';
$apiKey = 'password';
$client = new SoapClient('http://ourhost.com/api/v2_soap/?wsdl');
// We authenticate ourselves and get a session token id
$sessionId = $client->login($apiUser, $apiKey);
```

To get a session token ID in REST, we need to execute the following steps:

```
$callbackUrl = "http://magento.localhost.com/oauth_admin.php";
$temporaryCredentialsRequestUrl = "http://magento.localhost.com/oauth/
initiate?oauth_callback=" . urlencode($callbackUrl);
$adminAuthorizationUrl = 'http://magento.localhost.com/admin/oAuth_
authorize';
$accessTokenRequestUrl = 'http://magento.localhost.com/oauth/token';
$apiUrl = 'http://magento.localhost.com/api/rest';
$consumerKey = 'yourconsumerkey';
$consumerSecret = 'yourconsumersecret';

session_start();

$authType = ($_SESSION['state'] == 2) ? OAUTH_AUTH_TYPE_AUTHORIZATION
: OAUTH_AUTH_TYPE_URI;
$oauthClient = new OAuth($consumerKey, $consumerSecret, OAUTH_SIG_
METHOD_HMACSHA1, $authType);

$oauthClient->setToken($_SESSION['token'], $_SESSION['secret']);
```

Loading and reading data

The `Mage_Catalog` module product endpoint has the following exposed methods that we can use to manage products:

- `catalog_product.currentStore`: This sets/gets the current store view
- `catalog_product.list`: This retrieves products list using filters
- `catalog_product.info`: This retrieves a product
- `catalog_product.create`: This creates a new product
- `catalog_product.update`: This updates a product
- `catalog_product.setSpecialPrice`: This sets a special price for a product
- `catalog_product.getSpecialPrice`: This gets a special price for a product
- `catalog_product.delete`: This deletes a product

Right now, the functions that are of particular interest for us are `catalog_product.list` and `catalog_product.info`. Let's see how we can use the API to retrieve product data from our staging store.

To retrieve product data from our staging store in XML-RPC, execute the following code:

```
...
$result = $client->call($sessionId, 'catalog_product.list');
print_r ($result);
...
```

To retrieve product data from our staging store in SOAPv2, execute the following code:

```
...
$result = $client->catalogProductList($sessionId);
print_r($result);
...
```

To retrieve product data from our staging store in REST, execute the following code:

```
...
$resourceUrl = $apiUrl . "/products";
$oauthClient->fetch($resourceUrl, array(), 'GET', array('Content-Type'
=> 'application/json'));
$productsList = json_decode($oauthClient->getLastResponse());
...
```

Regardless of the protocol, we will get back a list of all the products' SKUs, but what if we want to filter that product list based on an attribute? Well, Magento lists functions that allow us to filter the product list based on an attribute by passing a parameter. Having said that, let's see how we can add filters to our product list call.

To add filters to our product list call in XML-RPC, execute the following code:

```
...
$result = $client->call('catalog_product.list', array($sessionId,
$filters);
print_r ($result);
...
```

To add filters to our product list call in SOAPv2, execute the following code:

```
...
$result = $client->catalogProductList($sessionId,$filters);
print_r($result);
...
```

With REST, things are not that simple and it is not possible to retrieve a product collection filtered by an attribute. However, we are able to retrieve all the products that belong to a specific category by executing the following code:

```
...
$categoryId = 3;
$resourceUrl = $apiUrl . "/products/category_id=" . categoryId ;
$oauthClient->fetch($resourceUrl, array(), 'GET', array('Content-Type'
=> 'application/json'));
$productsList = json_decode($oauthClient->getLastResponse());
...
```

Updating data

Now that we are able to retrieve product information from the Magento API, we can start updating the content of each product.

The `catalog_product.update` method will allow us to modify any of the product attributes; the function call takes the following parameters.

For updating data in XML-RPC, execute the following code:

```
...
$productId = 200;
$productData = array( 'sku' => 'changed_sku', 'name' => 'New Name',
'price' => 15.40 );
$result = $client->call($sessionId, 'catalog_product.update',
array($productId, $productData));
print_r($result);
...
```

For updating data in SOAPv2, execute the following code:

```
...
$productId = 200;
$productData = array( 'sku' => 'changed_sku', 'name' => 'New Name',
'price' => 15.40 );
$result = $client->catalogProductUpdate($sessionId, array($productId,
$productData));
print_r($result);
...
```

For updating data in REST, execute the following code:

```
...
$productData = json_encode(array(
    'type_id'           => 'simple',
    'attribute_set_id'  => 4,
    'sku'               => 'simple' . uniqid(),
    'weight'            => 10,
    'status'            => 1,
    'visibility'        => 4,
    'name'              => 'Test Product',
    'description'       => 'Description',
    'short_description' => 'Short Description',
    'price'             => 29.99,
    'tax_class_id'      => 2,
));
$oauthClient->fetch($resourceUrl, $productData, OAUTH_HTTP_METHOD_
POST, array('Content-Type' => 'application/json'));
$updatedProduct = json_decode($oauthClient->getLastResponseInfo());
...
```

Deleting a product

Deleting products by using the API is very simple and probably one of the most common operations.

For deleting products in XML-RPC, execute the following code:

```
...
$productId = 200;
$result = $client->call($sessionId, 'catalog_product.delete',
$productId);
print_r($result);
...
```

For deleting products in SOAPv2, execute the following code:

```
...
$productId = 200;
$result = $client->catalogProductDelete($sessionId, $productId);
print_r($result);
...
```

For deleting the code in REST, execute the following code:

```
...
$productData = json_encode(array(
    'id'            => 4
));
$oauthClient->fetch($resourceUrl, $productData, OAUTH_HTTP_METHOD_
DELETE, array('Content-Type' => 'application/json'));
$updatedProduct = json_decode($oauthClient->getLastResponseInfo());
...
```

Extending the API

Now that we have a basic understanding of how to use the Magento Core API, we can proceed to extend and add our own custom functionality. In order to add new API functionality, we have to modify/create the following files:

- `wsdl.xml`
- `api.xml`
- `api.php`

In order to make our registries accessible for third-party systems, we need to create and expose the following functions:

- `giftregistry_registry.list`: This retrieves a list of all the registry IDs and takes an optional customer ID parameter
- `giftregistry_registry.info`: This retrieves all the registry information and takes a required `registry_id` parameter
- `giftregistry_item.list`: This retrieves a list of all the registry item IDs associated to a registry and takes a required `registry_id` parameter
- `giftregistry_item.info`: This retrieves the product and detailed information of a registry item and takes one required `item_id` parameter

So far, we have only added reading operations. Let's now try to include API methods for updating, deleting, and creating registries and registry items.

 To see the answer with the complete code and full breakdown, visit `http://www.magedevguide.com/`.

Our first step is to implement the API class and the required functions:

1. Navigate to the `Model` directory.
2. Create a new class called `Api.php` and place the following placeholder content inside it:

    The file location is `app/code/local/Mdg/Giftregistry/Model/Api.php`.

    ```php
    <?php
    class Mdg_Giftregisty_Model_Api extends Mage_Api_Model_Resource_
    Abstract
    {
        public function getRegistryList($customerId = null)
        {

        }

        public function getRegistryInfo($registryId)
        {

        }

        public function getRegistryItems($registryId)
        {

        }

        public function getRegistryItemInfo($registryItemId)
        {

        }
    }
    ```

3. Create a new directory called `Api/`.
4. Inside `Api/` create a new class called `V2.php` and place the following placeholder content inside it:

    The file location is `app/code/local/Mdg/Giftregistry/Model/Api/V2.php`.

    ```php
    <?php
    class Mdg_Giftregisty_Model_Api_V2 extends Mdg_Giftregisty_Model_
    Api
    {

    }
    ```

The first thing you might notice is that the V2.php file is extending the API class we just created. The only difference is that the V2 class is used by the SOAP_v2 protocol, while the regular API class is used for all other requests.

Let's update the API class with the following working code:

The file location is app/code/local/Mdg/Giftregistry/Model/Api.php.

```php
<?php
class Mdg_Giftregisty_Model_Api extends Mage_Api_Model_Resource_
Abstract
{
    public function getRegistryList($customerId = null)
    {
        $registryCollection = Mage::getModel('mdg_giftregistry/
entity')->getCollection();
        if(!is_null($customerId))
        {
            $registryCollection->addFieldToFilter('customer_id',
$customerId);
        }
        return $registryCollection;
    }

    public function getRegistryInfo($registryId)
    {
        if(!is_null($registryId))
        {
            $registry = Mage::getModel('mdg_giftregistry/entity')-
>load($registryId);
            if($registry)
            {
                return $registry;
            } else {
             return false;
          }
        } else {
            return false;
        }
    }

    public function getRegistryItems($registryId)
    {
        if(!is_null($registryId))
        {
```

```
            $registryItems = Mage::getModel('mdg_giftregistry/item')-
>getCollection();
            $registryItems->addFieldToFilter('registry_id',
$registryId);
         Return $registryItems;
       } else {
          return false;
       }
    }


    public function getRegistryItemInfo($registryItemId)
    {
       if(!is_null($registryItemId))
       {
          $registryItem = Mage::getModel('mdg_giftregistry/item')-
>load($registryItemId);
          if($registryItem){
              return $registryItem;
          } else {
           return false;
          }
       } else {
          return false;
       }
    }
}
```

As we can see from the preceding code, we are not doing anything new. Each function is in charge of loading either a collection of Magento objects or a specific object based on the required parameters.

In order to expose this new function to the Magento API, we need to configure the XML files we created before. Let's start by updating the api.xml file:

1. Open the api.xml file.

2. Add the following XML code:

   The file location is app/code/local/Mdg/Giftregistry/etc/api.xml.

   ```
   <?xml version="1.0"?>
   <config>
       <api>
           <resources>
               <giftregistry_registry translate="title" module="mdg_
   giftregistry">
                   <model>mdg_giftregistry/api</model>
   ```

```
                    <title>Mdg Giftregistry Registry functions</title>
                    <methods>
                        <list translate="title" module="mdg_
giftregistry">
                            <title>getRegistryList</title>
                            <method>getRegistryList</method>
                        </list>
                        <info translate="title" module="mdg_
giftregistry">
                            <title>getRegistryInfo</title>
                            <method>getRegistryInfo</method>
                        </info>
                    </methods>
                </giftregistry_registry>
                <giftregistry_item translate="title" module="mdg_
giftregistry">
                    <model>mdg_giftregistry/api</model>
                    <title>Mdg Giftregistry Registry Items functions</
title>
                    <methods>
                        <list translate="title" module="mdg_
giftregistry">
                            <title>getRegistryItems</title>
                            <method>getRegistryItems</method>
                        </list>
                        <info translate="title" module="mdg_
giftregistry">
                            <title>getRegistryItemInfo</title>
                            <method>getRegistryItemInfo</method>
                        </info>
                    </methods>
                </giftregistry_item>
            </resources>
            <resources_alias>
                <giftregistry_registry>giftregistry_registry</
giftregistry_registry>
                <giftregistry_item>giftregistry_item</giftregistry_
item>
            </resources_alias>
            <v2>
                <resources_function_prefix>
                    <giftregistry_registry>giftregistry_registry</
giftregistry_registry>
                    <giftregistry_item>giftregistry_item</
giftregistry_item>
```

```
                </resources_function_prefix>
            </v2>
        </api>
</config>
```

There is one more file we need to update to make sure the SOAP adapters pick up our new API functions:

1. Open the `wsdl.xml` file.
2. Since the `wsdl.xml` file is normally very long in extent, we will break it down in several places. Let's start by defining the skeleton of the `wsdl.xml` file:

    The file location is `app/code/local/Mdg/Giftregistry/etc/wsdl.xml`.

```xml
<?xml version="1.0" encoding="UTF-8"?>
<definitions xmlns:typens="urn:{{var wsdl.name}}"
xmlns:xsd="http://www.w3.org/2001/XMLSchema" xmlns:soap="http://
schemas.xmlsoap.org/wsdl/soap/"
            xmlns:soapenc="http://schemas.xmlsoap.org/soap/
encoding/" xmlns:wsdl="http://schemas.xmlsoap.org/wsdl/"
xmlns="http://schemas.xmlsoap.org/wsdl/"
            name="{{var wsdl.name}}" targetNamespace="urn:{{var
wsdl.name}}">
    <types>

    </types>
    <message name="gitregistryRegistryListRequest">

    </message>
    <portType name="{{var wsdl.handler}}PortType">

    </portType>
    <binding name="{{var wsdl.handler}}Binding" type="typens:{{var
wsdl.handler}}PortType">
        <soap:binding style="rpc" transport="http://schemas.
xmlsoap.org/soap/http" />

    </binding>
    <service name="{{var wsdl.name}}Service">
        <port name="{{var wsdl.handler}}Port"
binding="typens:{{var wsdl.handler}}Binding">
            <soap:address location="{{var wsdl.url}}" />
        </port>
    </service>
</definitions>
```

3. This is the basic placeholder. We have all the main nodes that we defined at the beginning of the chapter. The first thing that we have to define is the custom data types that our API will use:

The file location is `app/code/local/Mdg/Giftregistry/etc/wsdl.xml`.

```
...
<schema xmlns="http://www.w3.org/2001/XMLSchema"
targetNamespace="urn:Magento">
            <import namespace="http://schemas.xmlsoap.org/soap/
encoding/" schemaLocation="http://schemas.xmlsoap.org/soap/
encoding/"/>
            <complexType name="giftRegistryEntity">
                <all>
                    <element name="entity_id" type="xsd:integer"
minOccurs="0" />
                    <element name="customer_id" type="xsd:integer"
minOccurs="0" />
                    <element name="type_id" type="xsd:integer"
minOccurs="0" />
                    <element name="website_id" type="xsd:integer"
minOccurs="0" />
                    <element name="event_date" type="xsd:string"
minOccurs="0" />
                    <element name="event_country"
type="xsd:string" minOccurs="0" />
                    <element name="event_location"
type="xsd:string" minOccurs="0" />
                </all>
            </complexType>
            <complexType name="giftRegistryEntityArray">
                <complexContent>
                    <restriction base="soapenc:Array">
                        <attribute ref="soapenc:arrayType" wsdl:ar
rayType="typens:giftRegistryEntity[]" />
                    </restriction>
                </complexContent>
            </complexType>
            <complexType name="registryItemsEntity">
                <all>
                    <element name="item_id" type="xsd:integer"
minOccurs="0" />
                    <element name="registry_id" type="xsd:integer"
minOccurs="0" />
                    <element name="product_id" type="xsd:integer"
minOccurs="0" />
                </all>
```

```
            </complexType>
            <complexType name="registryItemsArray">
                <complexContent>
                    <restriction base="soapenc:Array">
                        <attribute ref="soapenc:arrayType" wsdl:ar
rayType="typens:registryItemsEntity[]" />
                    </restriction>
                </complexContent>
            </complexType>
        </schema>
    ...
```

> Complex data types allow us to map which attributes and objects are transmitted through the API.

4. Messages allow us to define which of the complex types are transmitted
    on each API call request and response. Let's proceed to add the respective
    messages in our wsdl.xml:

    The file location is app/code/local/Mdg/Giftregistry/etc/wsdl.xml.

```
    ...
    <message name="gitregistryRegistryListRequest">
        <part name="sessionId" type="xsd:string" />
        <part name="customerId" type="xsd:integer"/>
    </message>
    <message name="gitregistryRegistryListResponse">
        <part name="result" type="typens:giftRegistryEntityArray"
/>
    </message>
    <message name="gitregistryRegistryInfoRequest">
        <part name="sessionId" type="xsd:string" />
        <part name="registryId" type="xsd:integer"/>
    </message>
    <message name="gitregistryRegistryInfoResponse">
        <part name="result" type="typens:giftRegistryEntity" />
    </message>
    <message name="gitregistryItemListRequest">
        <part name="sessionId" type="xsd:string" />
        <part name="registryId" type="xsd:integer"/>
    </message>
    <message name="gitregistryItemListResponse">
        <part name="result" type="typens:registryItemsArray" />
    </message>
    <message name="gitregistryItemInfoRequest">
```

```
        <part name="sessionId" type="xsd:string" />
        <part name="registryItemId" type="xsd:integer"/>
    </message>
    <message name="gitregistryItemInfoResponse">
        <part name="result" type="typens:registryItemsEntity" />
    </message>
...
```

5. One important thing to notice is that each request message will always include a `sessionId` property that is used to validate and authenticate each request, whereas the response is used to specify which complied data types or values are returned:

   The file location is `app/code/local/Mdg/Giftregistry/etc/wsdl.xml`.

```
...
    <portType name="{{var wsdl.handler}}PortType">
        <operation name="giftregistryRegistryList">
            <documentation>Get Registries List</documentation>
            <input message="typens:gitregistryRegistryListRequest"
/>
            <output message="typens:gitregistryRegistryListRespon
se" />
        </operation>
        <operation name="giftregistryRegistryInfo">
            <documentation>Get Registry Info</documentation>
            <input message="typens:gitregistryRegistryInfoRequest"
/>
            <output message="typens:gitregistryRegistryInfoRespon
se" />
        </operation>
        <operation name="giftregistryItemList">
            <documentation>getAllProductsInfo</documentation>
            <input message="typens:gitregistryItemListRequest" />
            <output message="typens:gitregistryItemListResponse"
/>
        </operation>
        <operation name="giftregistryItemInfo">
            <documentation>getAllProductsInfo</documentation>
            <input message="typens:gitregistryItemInfoRequest" />
            <output message="typens:gitregistryItemInfoResponse"
/>
        </operation>
    </portType>
...
```

6. The next thing that is required for properly adding the new API endpoints is to define the bindings, which are used to specify which methods are exposed:

The file location is `app/code/local/Mdg/Giftregistry/etc/wsdl.xml`.

```
...
<operation name="giftregistryRegistryList">
        <soap:operation soapAction="urn:{{var wsdl.handler}}
Action" />
        <input>
            <soap:body namespace="urn:{{var wsdl.name}}"
use="encoded" encodingStyle="http://schemas.xmlsoap.org/soap/
encoding/" />
        </input>
        <output>
            <soap:body namespace="urn:{{var wsdl.name}}"
use="encoded" encodingStyle="http://schemas.xmlsoap.org/soap/
encoding/" />
        </output>
    </operation>
    <operation name="giftregistryRegistryInfo">
        <soap:operation soapAction="urn:{{var wsdl.handler}}
Action" />
        <input>
            <soap:body namespace="urn:{{var wsdl.name}}"
use="encoded" encodingStyle="http://schemas.xmlsoap.org/soap/
encoding/" />
        </input>
        <output>
            <soap:body namespace="urn:{{var wsdl.name}}"
use="encoded" encodingStyle="http://schemas.xmlsoap.org/soap/
encoding/" />
        </output>
    </operation>
    <operation name="giftregistryItemList">
        <soap:operation soapAction="urn:{{var wsdl.handler}}
Action" />
        <input>
            <soap:body namespace="urn:{{var wsdl.name}}"
use="encoded" encodingStyle="http://schemas.xmlsoap.org/soap/
encoding/" />
        </input>
        <output>
            <soap:body namespace="urn:{{var wsdl.name}}"
use="encoded" encodingStyle="http://schemas.xmlsoap.org/soap/
encoding/" />
        </output>
```

```
        </operation>
        <operation name="giftregistryInfoList">
            <soap:operation soapAction="urn:{{var wsdl.handler}}
Action" />
            <input>
                <soap:body namespace="urn:{{var wsdl.name}}"
use="encoded" encodingStyle="http://schemas.xmlsoap.org/soap/
encoding/" />
            </input>
            <output>
                <soap:body namespace="urn:{{var wsdl.name}}"
use="encoded" encodingStyle="http://schemas.xmlsoap.org/soap/
encoding/" />
            </output>
        </operation>
    ...
```

 You can see the complete wsdl.xml in one piece at
http://magedevguide.com/chapter6/wsdl.

Even after we broke it down, the WSDL code can still seem overwhelming, and to be honest, it took me some time to get used to such a massive XML file. So if you feel or are feeling it is too much, just take it one step at a time.

Extending the REST API

So far, we have only worked on extending the SOAP and XML-RPC parts of the API. The process involved in extending the RESTful API is slightly different.

 The REST API was introduced with Magento Community
Edition 1.7 and Enterprise Edition 1.12.

In order to expose the new API methods to the REST API, we need to create a new file called api2.xml. The configuration on this file is a little more complex than the normal api.xml, so we will break it down after adding the full code:

1. Create a new file called api2.xml under the etc/ folder.

2. Open api2.xml.

3. Copy the following code:

    The file location is app/code/local/Mdg/Giftregistry/etc/api2.xml.

    ```
    <?xml version="1.0"?>
    <config>
    ```

```
<api2>
    <resource_groups>
        <giftregistry translate="title" module="mdg_
giftregistry">
            <title>MDG GiftRegistry API calls</title>
            <sort_order>30</sort_order>
            <children>
                <giftregistry_registry translate="title"
module="mdg_giftregistry">
                    <title>Gift Registries</title>
                    <sort_order>50</sort_order>
                </giftregistry_registry>
                <giftregistry_item translate="title"
module="mdg_giftregistry">
                    <title>Gift Registry Items</title>
                    <sort_order>50</sort_order>
                </giftregistry_item>
            </children>
        </giftregistry>
    </resource_groups>
    <resources>
        <giftregistryregistry translate="title" module="mdg_
giftregistry">
            <group>giftregistry_registry</group>
            <model>mdg_giftregistry/api_registry</model>
            <working_model>mdg_giftregistry/api_registry</
working_model>
            <title>Gift Registry</title>
            <sort_order>10</sort_order>
            <privileges>
                <admin>
                    <create>1</create>
                    <retrieve>1</retrieve>
                    <update>1</update>
                    <delete>1</delete>
                </admin>
            </privileges>
            <attributes translate="product_count" module="mdg_
giftregistry">
                <registry_list>Registry List</registry_list>
                <registry>Registry</registry>
                <item_list>Item List</item_list>
                <item>Item</item>
            </attributes>
            <entity_only_attributes>
            </entity_only_attributes>
```

```
<exclude_attributes>
</exclude_attributes>
<routes>
    <route_registry_list>
        <route>/mdg/registry/list</route>
        <action_type>collection</action_type>
    </route_registry_list>
    <route_registry_entity>
        <route>/mdg/registry/:registry_id</route>
        <action_type>entity</action_type>
    </route_registry_entity>
    <route_registry_list>
        <route>/mdg/registry_item/list</route>
        <action_type>collection</action_type>
    </route_registry_list>
    <route_registry_list>
        <route>/mdg/registry_item/:item_id</route>
        <action_type>entity</action_type>
    </route_registry_list>
</routes>
<versions>1</versions>
                </giftregistryregistry>
            </resources>
        </api2>
    </config>
```

One important thing to notice is that we are defining a route node inside this configuration file. This is treated by Magento as a frontend route and it is used to access the RESTful `api` function. Also notice that we don't need to create a new controller for this to work.

Now, we also need to include a new class to handle the REST requests, and implement each of the defined privileges:

1. Create a new class called `V1.php` under `Model/Api/Registry/Rest/Admin`.

2. Open the `V1.php` class and copy the following code:

   The file location is `app/code/local/Mdg/Giftregistry/Model/Api/Registry/Rest/Admin/V1.php`.

   ```php
   <?php

   class Mdg_Giftregistry_Model_Api_Registry_Rest_Admin_V1 extends
   Mage_Catalog_Model_Api2_Product_Rest {
       /**
        * @return stdClass
        */
   ```

```
    protected function _retrieve()
    {
        $registryCollection = Mage::getModel('mdg_giftregistry/
entity')->getCollection();
        return $registryCollection;
    }
}
```

Securing the API

Securing our API is already a part of the process of creating our module and it is also handled by the configuration. The way Magento restricts access to its API is by using ACL.

As we learned before, these ACL allow us to set up roles with access to different parts of the API. Now, what we have to do is make our new custom functions available to the ACL:

1. Open the `api.xml` file.

2. Add the following code after the `</v2>` node:

    The file location is `app/code/local/Mdg/Giftregistry/etc/api.xml`.

```xml
<acl>
    <resources>
        <giftregistry translate="title" module="mdg_giftregistry">
            <title>MDG Gift Registry</title>
            <sort_order>1</sort_order>
            <registry translate="title" module="mdg_giftregistry">
                <title>MDG Gift Registry</title>
                <list translate="title" module="mdg_giftregistry">
                    <title>List Available Registries</title>
                </list>
                <info translate="title" module="mdg_giftregistry">
                    <title>Retrieve registry data</title>
                </info>
            </registry>
            <item translate="title" module="mdg_giftregistry">
                <title>MDG Gift Registry Item</title>
                <list translate="title" module="mdg_giftregistry">
                    <title>List Available Items inside a
registry</title>
                </list>
                <info translate="title" module="mdg_giftregistry">
                    <title>Retrieve registry item data</title>
```

```
          </info>
        </item>
      </giftregistry>
    </resources>
  </acl>
```

Summary

In previous chapters, we learned how to extend Magento to add new functionality for both store owners and customers; knowing how to extend and work with the Magento API opens a world of possibilities.

By using the API, we can integrate Magento with third-party systems like ERP and points of sale; both by importing and exporting data.

In the next chapter we will learn how to properly build a test for all the code we have built so far, and we will also explore multiple testing frameworks.

Testing and Quality Assurance

So far, we have covered:

- The Magento fundamentals
- Frontend development
- Backend development
- Extending and working with the API

However, we omitted a critical step of the development of any extension or custom code: testing and quality assurance.

Despite the fact that Magento is a very complex and large platform, there is no included/integrated unit test suite on versions previous to Magento2.

For that reason, proper testing and quality assurance is often overlooked by most Magento developers either by lack of information or because of the large overhead of some of the testing tools, and while there are not many tools available for running a proper test with Magento, the ones that exist are of very high quality.

In this chapter, we will take a look at the different options available for testing our Magento code, and we will also build some very basic tests for our custom extension.

So let's go over the topics covered in this chapter:

- The different testing frameworks and tools available for Magento
- The importance of testing our Magento code
- How to set up, install, and use Ecomdev PHPUnit extension
- How to set up, install, and use Magento Mink for running functional tests

Testing Magento

Before we start writing any test, it is important that we understand the concepts related to testing and more particularly to each of the available methodologies.

Unit testing

The idea behind unit testing is writing tests for certain areas (units) of our code, so we can verify that the code works as expected and that function is returning expected values.

> *Unit testing is a method by which individual units of source code, sets of one or more computer program modules together with associated control data, usage procedures, and operating procedures, are tested to determine if they are fit for use.*

Another advantage of writing unit tests is that by performing the test, so we are more likely to write code that is easier to test.

This means our code tends to be broken down into smaller but more specialized functions as we continue to write more and more tests. We start building a test suite that can be run against our codebase every time we introduce changes or functionalities; this is known as regression testing.

Regression testing

Regression testing mostly refers to the practice of re-running existing test suites after making code changes to check whether a new functionality is not also introducing new bugs.

> *Regression testing is any type of software testing that seeks to uncover new software bugs, or regressions, in existing functional and non-functional areas of a system after changes, such as enhancements, patches, or configuration changes, have been made to them.*

In the particular case of a Magento store or any e-commerce site, we want to perform regression testing on critical features of the store such as checkout, customer registration, adding to the cart, and so on.

Functional tests

Functional testing is more concerned with testing that the application returns the appropriate output based on a specific input, rather than what happens internally.

> *Functional testing is a type of black-box testing that bases its test cases on the specifications of the software component under test. Functions are tested by feeding them input and examining the output, and internal program structure is rarely considered.*

This is especially important for e-commerce websites like ours where we want to test the site as the customer would experience it.

TDD

One testing methodology that has gained popularity in recent years and that is now coming to Magento is known as **Test-driven development** (TDD).

> *Test-driven development (TDD) is a software development process that relies on the repetition of a very short development cycle: first the developer writes an (initially failing) automated test case that defines a desired improvement or new function, then produces the minimum amount of code to pass that test and finally refactors the new code to acceptable standards.*

The basic concept behind TDD is to first write a failing test and then write code to pass the test; this generates very short development cycles and helps to streamline the code.

Ideally, you want to start the development of your modules and extensions by using TDD in Magento. We omitted this in previous chapters due to the fact that it would add unnecessary complexity and confuse the reader.

 For a full tutorial on TDD with Magento from scratch, visit `http://magedevguide.com/getting-started-with-tdd`.

Tools and testing frameworks

As mentioned before, there are several frameworks and tools available for testing PHP code and Magento code. Let's get to know each one of them a little better:

- `Ecomdev_PHPUnit`: This extension is just amazing; the developers at Ecomdev created an extension that integrates PHPUnit with Magento and also adds Magento-specific assertions to PHPUnit, all without having to modify core files or affect the database.

- `Magento_Mink`: Mink is a PHP library for the Behat framework that allows you to write functional and acceptance tests; Mink allows writing tests that simulate user behavior and browser interaction.

- `Magento_TAF`: `Magento_TAF` stands for Magento Test Automation Framework, which is the official testing tool provided by Magento. `Magento_TAF` includes over 1,000 functional tests and is very powerful. Unfortunately, it has a major drawback; it has a large overhead and steep learning curve.

Unit testing with PHPUnit

Before `Ecomdev_PHPUnit`, testing Magento with PHPUnit was problematic and really not very practical from the different methods that were available. Almost all required core code modifications or developers had to jump through hoops to set up basic PHPUnits.

Installing Ecomdev_PHPUnit

The easiest way to install `Ecomdev_PHPUnit` is to grab a copy directly from the GitHub repository. Let's write the following command on our console:

```
git clone git://github.com/IvanChepurnyi/EcomDev_PHPUnit.git
```

Now copy the file over to your Magento root folder.

 Composer and Modman are alternative options available for installation. For more information on each, please visit http://magedevguide.com/module-managers.

Finally, we need to set the configuration to instruct the PHPUnit extension which database to use; `local.xml.phpunit` is a new file added by `Ecomdev_PHPUnit`. This file holds all the extension-specific configuration and specifies the name of the test database.

The file location is `app/etc/local.xml.phpunit`. Refer to the following code:

```xml
<?xml version="1.0"?>
<config>
    <global>
        <resources>
            <default_setup>
                <connection>
                    <dbname><![CDATA[magento_unit_tests]]></dbname>
                </connection>
            </default_setup>
        </resources>
    </global>
    <default>
        <web>
            <seo>
                <use_rewrites>1</use_rewrites>
            </seo>
            <secure>
                <base_url>[change me]</base_url>
            </secure>
            <unsecure>
                <base_url>[change me]</base_url>
            </unsecure>
            <url>
                <redirect_to_base>0</redirect_to_base>
            </url>
        </web>
    </default>
    <phpunit>
        <allow_same_db>0</allow_same_db>
    </phpunit>
</config>
```

You will need to create a new database for running tests and replace the example configuration values in the `local.xml.phpunit` file.

By default, this extension does not allow you to run the test on the same database; keeping the test database separate from the development and production allows us to run our test with confidence.

Setting up the configuration for our extension

Now that we have the PHPUnit extension installed and set up, we need to prepare our gift registry extension for running unit tests. Follow these steps:

1. Open the Gift Registry extension, `config.xml` file

2. Add the following code (the file location is `app/code/local/Mdg/Giftregistry/etc/config.xml`):

```
...
<phpunit>
        <suite>
            <modules>
                    <Mdg_Giftregistry/>
            </modules>
        </suite>
</phpunit>
...
```

This new configuration node allows the PHPUnit extension to recognize the extension and run the matching tests.

We also need to create a new directory called `Test` that we will use to place all our test files. One of the advantages about using `Ecomdev_PHPUnit` over previous methods is that this extension follows the Magento standards.

This means we have to keep the same module directory structure inside the `Test` folder:

```
Test/
Model/
Block/
Helper/
Controller/
Config/
```

Based on that, the naming convention for each `Test` case class would be `[Namespace]_[Module Name]_Test_[Group Directory]_[Entity Name]`.

Each `Test` class must extend one of the following three base `Test` classes:

- `EcomDev_PHPUnit_Test_Case`: This class is used for testing helpers, models, and blocks

- `EcomDev_PHPUnit_Test_Case_Config`: This class is used for testing the module configuration

- `EcomDev_PHPUnit_Test_Case_Controller`: This class is used for testing the layout rendering process and the controller logic

Anatomy of a Test case

Before jumping ahead and trying to create our first test, let's break down one of the examples provided by `Ecomdev_PHPUnit`:

```php
<?php
class EcomDev_Example_Test_Model_Product extends EcomDev_PHPUnit_Test_
Case
{
    /**
     * Product price calculation test
     *
     * @test
     * @loadFixture
     * @doNotIndexAll
     * @dataProvider dataProvider
     */
    public function priceCalculation($productId, $storeId)
    {
        $storeId = Mage::app()->getStore($storeId)->getId();
        $product = Mage::getModel('catalog/product')
            ->setStoreId($storeId)
            ->load($productId);
        $expected = $this->expected('%s-%s', $productId, $storeId);
        $this->assertEquals(
            $expected->getFinalPrice(),
            $product->getFinalPrice()
        );
        $this->assertEquals(
            $expected->getPrice(),
            $product->getPrice()
        );
    }
}
```

The first important thing to notice in the example `test` class is the comment annotations:

```php
...
/**
     * Product price calculation test
     *
     * @test
     * @loadFixture
     * @doNotIndexAll
     * @dataProvider dataProvider
     */
...
```

These annotations are used by the PHPUnit extension to identify which of the class functions are tests, and also, they allow us to set up specific settings for running each test. Let's take a look at some of the available annotations:

- `@test`: This annotation identifies a class function as a PHPUnit test
- `@loadFixture`: This annotation specifies the use of fixtures
- `@loadExpectation`: This annotation specifies the use of expectations
- `@doNotIndexAll`: By adding this annotation, we are telling the PHPUnit tests that they should not run any index after loading the fixtures
- `@doNotIndex [index_code]`: By adding this annotation, we can instruct PHPUnit not to run a specific index

So now, you are probably a bit confused. Fixtures? Expectations? What are they?

Following is a little description on Fixtures and Expectations:

- **Fixtures**: Fixtures are **yet another markup language (YAML)** files that represent database or configuration entities
- **Expectations**: Expectations are useful if we don't want to have hard-coded values in our tests and are also specified in YAML values

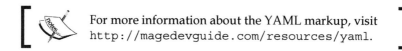

For more information about the YAML markup, visit `http://magedevguide.com/resources/yaml`.

So, as we see, fixtures provide the data for the tests to process, and the expectations are used to check if the results returned by the test are what we are expecting to see.

Fixtures and expectations are stored inside each `Test` type directory. Following the example earlier, we would have a new directory called `Product/`. Inside it, we need a new directory for expectations and one for our fixtures.

Let's take a look at the revised folder structure:

```
Test/
Model/
  Product.php
  Product/
    expectations/
    fixtures/
Block/
Helper/
Controller/
Config/
```

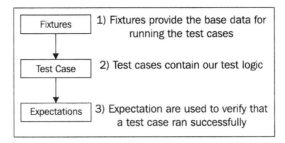

1) Fixtures provide the base data for running the test cases

2) Test cases contain our test logic

3) Expectation are used to verify that a test case ran successfully

Creating a unit test

For our first UnitTest, let's create a very basic test that allows us to test the Gift Registry Models that we previously created.

As we mentioned before, `Ecomdev_PHPUnit` uses a separate database for running all the tests; for this, we need to create a new fixture that will provide all the data for our test case. Follow these steps:

1. Open the `Test/Model` folder.

2. Create a new folder called `Registry`.

3. Inside the `Registry` folder, create a new folder called `fixtures`.

4. Create a new file called `registryList.yaml` and paste the following code in it (the file location is `app/code/local/Mdg/Giftregistry/Test/Model/fixtures/registryList.yaml`):

```
website: # Initialize websites
  - website_id: 2
    code: default
    name: Test Website
    default_group_id: 2
group: # Initializes store groups
  - group_id: 2
    website_id: 2
    name: Test Store Group
    default_store_id: 2
    root_category_id: 2 # Default Category
store: # Initializes store views
  - store_id: 2
    website_id: 2
    group_id: 2
    code: default
    name: Default Test Store
    is_active: 1
```

```
eav:
    customer_customer:
      - entity_id: 1
        entity_type_id: 3
        website_id: 2
        email: test@magentotest.com
        group_id: 2
        store_id: 2
        is_active: 1
    mdg_giftregistry_entity:
      - entity_id: 1
        customer_id: 1
        type_id: 2
        website_id: 2
        event_date: 12/12/2012
        event_country: Canada
        event_location: Dundas Square
        created_at: 21/12/2012
      - entity_id: 2
        customer_id: 1
        type_id: 3
        website_id: 2
        event_date: 01/01/2013
        event_country: Canada
        event_location: Eaton Center
        created_at: 21/12/2012
```

It might not look like it, but we add a lot of information with this fixture. We will create the following fixture data:

- A website scope
- A store group
- A store view
- A customer record
- Two gift registries

By using fixtures, we are creating data on the fly that will be available for our test case. This gives us the consistency of running the test multiple times against the same data and the flexibility to easily change it.

Now, you might be wondering how the PHPUnit extension knows how to pair a Test case with a specific fixture.

There are two ways the extension loads fixtures: one is by specifying the fixture inside the comment annotations, or if the fixture name is not specified, the extension will search a fixture with same name as the `Test` case function being executed.

Knowing that, let's create our first `Test` case:

1. Navigate to the `Test/Model` folder.

2. Create a new `Test` class called `Registry.php`.

3. Add the following base code (the file location is `app/code/local/Mdg/Giftregistry/Test/Model/Registry.php`):

```php
<?php
class Mdg_Giftregistry_Test_Model_Registry extends EcomDev_
PHPUnit_Test_Case
{
    /**
     * Listing available registries
     *
     * @test
     * @loadFixture
     * @doNotIndexAll
     * @dataProvider dataProvider
     */
    public function registryList()
    {

    }
}
```

We just created the base function, but we haven't added any logic yet. Before doing that, let's take a look at what actually constitutes a `Test` case.

A `Test` case works by using assertions to evaluate and test our code. Assertions are special functions that our `Test` cases inherit from the parent `TestCase` class. Among the default assertions available, we have:

- `assertEquals()`
- `assertGreaterThan()`
- `assertGreaterThanOrEqual()`
- `assertLessThan()`
- `assertLessThanOrEqual()`
- `assertTrue()`

Now, these default assertions are great if we want to check variable's values; search for an array key, check attributes, and so on. But testing Magento code, using only these types of assertions, can prove difficult or even impossible. This is where `Ecomdev_PHPUnit` comes to the rescue.

Not only has this extension integrated PHPUnit with Magento cleanly, by following their standards, it also adds Magento-specific assertions to the PHPUnit tests. Let's take a look at some of the assertions added by the extension:

- `assertEventDispatched()`
- `assertBlockAlias()`
- `assertModelAlias()`
- `assertHelperAlias()`
- `assertModuleCodePool()`
- `assertModuleDepends()`
- `assertConfigNodeValue()`
- `assertLayoutFileExists()`

Those are only a few of the assertions available, and as you can see, they give a lot of power for building comprehensive tests.

Now that we know a little more about how PHPUnit `Test` cases work, let's proceed to creating our first Magento `Test` case:

1. Navigate to the `Registry.php` test case class that we created before.
2. Add the following code inside the `registryList()` function (the file location is `app/code/local/Mdg/Giftregistry/Test/Model/Registry.php`):

```
/**
 * Listing available registries
 *
 * @test
 * @loadFixture
 * @doNotIndexAll
 * @dataProvider dataProvider
 */
public function registryList()
{
    $registryList = Mage::getModel('mdg_giftregistry/entity')-
>getCollection();
    $this->assertEquals(
```

```
            2,
            $registryList->count()
        );
    }
```

This is a very basic test; the only thing that we are doing is loading a registry collection. In this case, all the registries are available, and then they run an assertion to check if the collection count matches.

However, this is not very useful. It would be even better if we were able to load only the registries that belong to a specific user (our test user) and check that collection size. That said, let's change the code a little bit:

The file location is `app/code/local/Mdg/Giftregistry/Test/Model/Registry.php`. Refer to the following code:

```
    /**
     * Listing available registries
     *
     * @test
     * @loadFixture
     * @doNotIndexAll
     * @dataProvider dataProvider
     */
    public function registryList()
    {
        $customerId = 1;
        $registryList = Mage::getModel('mdg_giftregistry/entity')
->getCollection()
->addFieldToFilter('customer_id', $customerId);
        $this->assertEquals(
            2,
            $registryList->count()
        );
    }
```

Just by changing a few lines of code, we created a test that allows checking whether our registry collections are working properly and if they are correctly linked to a customer record.

Run the following command in your shell:

```
$ phpunit
```

If everything went as expected, we should see the following output:

```
PHPUnit 3.4 by Sebastian Bergmann

.

Time: 1 second
Tests: 1, Assertions: 1, Failures 0
```

 You can also run $phpunit — colors for a nicer output.

Now, we only need a test to verify that the registry items are working properly:

1. Navigate to the `Registry.php` test case class that we created before.
2. Add the following code inside the `registryItemsList()` function (the file location is `app/code/local/Mdg/Giftregistry/Test/Model/Registry.php`):

```php
/**
 * Listing available items for a specific registry
 *
 * @test
 * @loadFixture
 * @doNotIndexAll
 * @dataProvider dataProvider
 */
public function registryItemsList()
{
    $customerId = 1;
    $registry   = Mage::getModel('mdg_giftregistry/entity')
->loadByCustomerId($customerId);

    $registryItems = $registry->getItems();
    $this->assertEquals(
        3,
        $registryItems->count()
    );
}
```

We will also need a new fixture for our new `Test` case:

1. Navigate to the `Test/Model` folder.
2. Open the `Registry` folder.

3. Create a new file called `registryItemsList.yaml` (the file location is `app/code/local/Mdg/Giftregistry/Test/Model/fixtures/registryItemsList.yaml`):

```yaml
website: # Initialize websites
  - website_id: 2
    code: default
    name: Test Website
    default_group_id: 2
group: # Initializes store groups
  - group_id: 2
    website_id: 2
    name: Test Store Group
    default_store_id: 2
    root_category_id: 2 # Default Category
store: # Initializes store views
  - store_id: 2
    website_id: 2
    group_id: 2
    code: default
    name: Default Test Store
    is_active: 1
eav:
  customer_customer:
    - entity_id: 1
      entity_type_id: 3
      website_id: 2
      email: test@magentotest.com
      group_id: 2
      store_id: 2
      is_active: 1
  mdg_giftregistry_entity:
    - entity_id: 1
      customer_id: 1
      type_id: 2
      website_id: 2
      event_date: 12/12/2012
      event_country: Canada
      event_location: Dundas Square
      created_at: 21/12/2012
  mdg_giftregistry_item:
    - item_id: 1
      registry_id: 1
      product_id: 1
    - item_id: 2
```

```
        registry_id: 1
        product_id: 2
     -  item_id: 3
        registry_id: 1
        product_id: 3
```

Let's run our test suite:

$phpunit --colors

We should see both tests passing:

```
PHPUnit 3.4 by Sebastian Bergmann

  .

Time: 4 second
Tests: 2, Assertions: 2, Failures 0
```

Finally, let's replace our hard-coded variables with proper expectations:

1. Navigate to the `Module Test/Model` folder.
2. Open the `Registry` folder.
3. Inside the `Registry` folder, create a new folder called `expectations`.
4. Create a new file called `registryList.yaml` (the file location is `app/code/ local/Mdg/Giftregistry/Test/Model/expectations/registryList. yaml`).

    ```
    count: 2
    ```

Wasn't that easy? Well, it was so easy that we will do it again for the `registryItemsList` test case:

1. Navigate to the `Module Test/Model` folder.
2. Open the `Registry` folder.
3. Create a new file called `registryItemsList.yaml` inside the `expectations` folder (the file location is `app/code/local/Mdg/Giftregistry/Test/ Model/expectations/registryItemsList.yaml`):

    ```
    count: 3
    ```

Finally, the last thing that we need to do is to update our `Test` case class to use the expectations. Make sure the update file has the following code (the file location is app/code/local/Mdg/Giftregistry/Test/Model/Registry.php):

```php
<?php
class Mdg_Giftregistry_Test_Model_Registry extends EcomDev_PHPUnit_
Test_Case
{
```

```
/**
 * Product price calculation test
 *
 * @test
 * @loadFixture
 * @doNotIndexAll
 * @dataProvider dataProvider
 */
public function registryList()
{
    $customerId = 1;
    $registryList = Mage::getModel('mdg_giftregistry/entity')
            ->getCollection()
            ->addFieldToFilter('customer_id', $customerId);
    $this->assertEquals(
        $this->_getExpectations()->getCount(),$this->_
getExpectations()->getCount(),
        $registryList->count()
    );
}
/**
 * Listing available items for a specific registry
 *
 * @test
 * @loadFixture
 * @doNotIndexAll
 * @dataProvider dataProvider
 */
public function registryItemsList()
{
    $customerId = 1;
    $registry    = Mage::getModel('mdg_giftregistry/entity')-
>loadByCustomerId($customerId);

    $registryItems = $registry->getItems();
    $this->assertEquals(
        $this->_getExpectations()->getCount(),
        $registryItems->count()
    );
}
}
```

The only change here is that we are replacing the hard-coded value inside our assertions with the expectations, values. If we ever need to make any changes, we don't need to change our code; we can just update the expectations and the fixtures.

Functional tests with Mink

So far, we have learned how to run unit tests against our code, and while unit tests are great for testing individual parts of our code and the logic, when it comes to large applications such as Magento, it is important to test from the user's perspective.

 Functional testing mostly involves black-box testing and is not concerned about the source code of the application.

In order to do that, we can use Mink. Mink is a simple PHP library that can virtualize a web browser. Mink works by using different drivers. Out of the box, it supports the following drivers:

- `GoutteDriver`: This is a pure-PHP headless browser written by the creator of Symfony framework
- `SahiDriver`: This is a new JS browser controller that is quickly replacing Selenium
- `ZombieDriver`: This is a browser emulator written in `Node.js` and currently is only limited to one browser (Chromium)
- `SeleniumDriver`: This is currently the most popular browser driver; the original version relies on a third-party server for running the tests
- `Selenium2Driver`: The current version of Selenium is fully supported in Python, Ruby, Java, and C#

Magento Mink installation and setup

Using Mink with Magento is extremely easy, thanks to Johann Reinke, who created a Magento extension that facilitates Mink integration with Magento.

We will install this extension using Modgit, a module manager inspired by Modman. Modgit allows us to deploy Magento extensions directly from a GitHub repository without creating symlinks.

Installing Modgit can be achieved with three lines of code:

```
wget -O modgit https://raw.github.com/jreinke/modgit/master/modgit
chmod +x modgit
sudo mv modgit /usr/local/bin
```

Wasn't that easy? Now we can proceed to install Magento Mink, for which we should thank Modgit that it is even easier:

1. Move to the Magento root directory.

2. Run the following commands:

   ```
   modgit init

   modgit -e README.md clone mink https://github.com/jreinke/magento-mink.git
   ```

That's it. Modgit will take care of installing the file for us directly from the GitHub repository.

Creating our first test

`Mink` tests are also stored inside the `Test` folder. Let's create the base skeleton of our `Mink` test class:

1. Navigate to the `Test` folder on our module root.

2. Create a new directory called `Mink`.

3. Inside the `Mink` directory, create a new PHP class called `Registry.php`.

4. Copy the following code (the file location is `app/code/local/Mdg/Giftregistry/Test/Mink/Registry.php`):

```php
<?php
class Mdg_Giftregistry_Test_Mink_Registry extends JR_Mink_Test_
Mink
{
    public function testAddProductToRegistry()
    {
        $this->section('TEST ADD PRODUCT TO REGISTRY');
        $this->setCurrentStore('default');
        $this->setDriver('goutte');
        $this->context();

        // Go to homepage
        $this->output($this->bold('Go To the Homepage'));
        $url = Mage::getStoreConfig('web/unsecure/base_url');
        $this->visit($url);
        $category = $this->find('css', '#nav .nav-1-1 a');
        if (!$category) {
            return false;
```

```
        }

        // Go to the Login page
        $loginUrl = $this->find('css', 'ul.links li.last a');
        if ($loginUrl) {
            $this->visit($loginUrl->getAttribute('href'));
        }

        $login = $this->find('css', '#email');
        $pwd = $this->find('css', '#pass');
        $submit = $this->find('css', '#send2');

        if ($login && $pwd && $submit) {
            $email = 'user@example.com';
            $password = 'password';
            $this->output(sprintf("Try to authenticate '%s' with
password '%s'", $email, $password));
            $login->setValue($email);
            $pwd->setValue($password);
            $submit->click();
            $this->attempt(
                $this->find('css', 'div.welcome-msg'),
                'Customer successfully logged in',
                'Error authenticating customer'
            );
        }

        // Go to the category page
        $this->output($this->bold('Go to the category list'));
        $this->visit($category->getAttribute('href'));
        $product = $this->find('css', '.category-products li.first
a');
        if (!$product) {
            return false;
        }

        // Go to product view
        $this->output($this->bold('Go to product view'));
        $this->visit($product->getAttribute('href'));
        $form = $this->find('css', '#product_registry_form');
        if ($form) {
            $addToCartUrl = $form->getAttribute('action');
            $this->visit($addToCartUrl);
            $this->attempt(
```

```
            $this->find('css', '#btn-add-giftregistry'),
            'Product added to gift registry successfully',
            'Error adding product to gift registry'
        );
    }
  }
}
```

Just at first glance, you can tell that this functional test is quite different from the unit tests that we built previously, and although it seems like a lot of code is quite simple. The previous test has been down in code blocks. Let's break down what the previous test is doing:

- Set up the browser driver and the current store
- Go to the home page and check for a valid category link
- Try to log in as a test user
- Go to a category page
- Open the first product on that category
- Try to add the product to the customer's gift registry

 This test makes few assumptions and is expecting a valid customer within an existing gift registry.

There are some considerations that we have to keep in mind when creating `Mink` tests:

- Each test class must extend `JR_Mink_Test_Mink`
- Each test function must start with the test keyword

Finally, the only thing that we have to perform is run our tests. We can do this by going to the command line and running the following command:

$ php shell/mink.php

If everything was successful, we should see something similar to the following output:

```
--------------------- SCRIPT START --------------------------------
Found 1 file
-------------- TEST ADD PRODUCT TO REGISTRY -----------------------
Switching to store 'default'
Now using Goutte driver
--------------------------------- CONTEXT ------------------------
-----------
```

```
website: base, store: default
Cache info:
config            Disabled  N/A       Configuration
layout            Disabled  N/A       Layouts
block_html        Disabled  N/A       Blocks HTML output
translate         Disabled  N/A       Translations
collections       Disabled  N/A       Collections Data
eav               Disabled  N/A       EAV types and attributes
config_api        Disabled  N/A       Web Services Configuration
config_api2       Disabled  N/A       Web Services Configuration
ecomdev_phpunit   Disabled  N/A       Unit Test Cases

Go To the Homepage [OK]
Try to authenticate user@example.com with password password [OK]
Go to the category list [OK]
Go to product view [OK]
Product added to gift registry successfully
```

Summary

In this chapter, we went over the basics of Magento testing. The purpose of this chapter was not to build complex tests or go in too deep, but rather get our feet wet and get a clear idea of what we can do to test our extensions.

We covered several important topics in this chapter, and by having proper test suites and tools, it can save us from future headaches and improve the quality of our code.

In the next and final chapter, we will learn how to package and distribute custom code and extensions.

8

Deployment and Distribution

Welcome to the last chapter of this book; we have come far and learned a lot along the way. By now, you should have a clear idea of everything involved in working and developing custom extensions for Magento.

Well, almost everything, as with any other Magento developer your code will eventually need to be promoted to production or maybe packaged for distribution; in this chapter we will see the different techniques, tools, and strategies that are available to us.

The final objective of this chapter is to give you the tools and skills to do deployments with confidence and with little to no downtime.

The road towards zero-downtime deployment

Deploying to production is probably one of the most dreaded tasks for developers, and more often than not, it will be improperly done.

But what is zero-downtime deployment? Well, it is to production with confidence, knowing the code is properly tested and ready, this is the ideal that all Magento developers should aspire to.

This is achieved not by a single process or tool but by a combination of techniques, standards, and tools. In this chapter we will learn the following:

- Distributing our extension through Magento Connect
- The role of version control systems in deployment
- Proper practices for branching and merging changes

Make it right from scratch

In the previous chapter, we learned how testing can not only enhance our workflow but also save us from future headaches. The unit tests, integration tests, and automated tools are all at our disposal to ensure that our code is properly tested.

Writing tests means more than just putting together a few tests and calling it done; we are responsible for thinking about all the possible edge cases that might affect our code and write tests for each of them.

Be sure that what you see is what you get

In the first chapter of this book, we dived right into setting up our development environment, which is a very important task. In order for us to guarantee that we are delivering quality and tested code, we must be able to develop and test our code in an environment as close to production as possible.

I'll illustrate the importance of this environment with an example on the early days of Magento. I heard it happened several times; developers worked on their local environments creating new extensions from scratch, they finished their development and tested on their local staging, and everything seemed to be working properly.

One of the commonly accepted workflows is:

- Starting development on the developer's local machine, which is running a virtual machine close to the production environment
- Testing and approving changes on a staging environment that is a close as possible copy of production
- Finally, deploying changes to the production environment

It was now time to promote their code to production and they confidently did so; of course it was working on local, hence it had to work on production, right? In these particular situations, it wasn't the case; what happened instead was that as soon the new code was loaded into production, the store crashed, saying the autoloader wasn't able to find the class.

What happened? Well, the problem was that the developers' local environment was Windows and the name of the extension folder was in CamelCase, for example `MyExtension`, but internally in the class names they were using the capitalized text (`Myextension`).

Now this will work just fine in Windows because the file does not distinguish between uppercase, capitalized, or lowercase folder names; while a Unix-based system like most of the web servers do make a distinction on the folder and file naming.

While this example may look silly, it illustrates quite well the need for a standardized development environment; there are so many parts and "moving pieces" in a Magento installation. A different version of PHP or an extra Apache module that is enabled in production but not staging can make a world of difference.

> Learn more about Magento naming conventions at
> `http://www.magedevguide.com/naming-conventions`.

Ready means ready

But when we say that our code is actually ready for production, what does ready really mean? Each developer might have a different definition of what ready and done actually mean. When working on a new module or extending Magento, we should always define what ready means for this particular feature/code.

So we are now getting somewhere, and we know that in order to pass the code to production, we have to do the following:

1. Test our code and make sure we have covered all the edge cases.
2. Make sure the code follows the standards and guidelines.
3. Make sure it has been tested and developed in an environment as close to the production as possible.

Version control system and deployment

Version control systems (**VCSs**) are the lifeblood of any developer, and while the field might be a bit divided among Git and SVN enthusiasts (no mention for you Mercurial guys), the basic functionalities are still the same.

Let's quickly go through the differences between each VCS, and their advantages and disadvantages.

SVN

This is a powerful system, and it has been around for quite some time and is very well known and widely used.

Subversion (SVN) is a centralized VCS; by this we mean that there is a single main source that is recognized as "Good", and all developers check out and push changes from and to this central source.

While this makes changes easier to track and maintain, it has a serious disadvantage. Being centralized also means that we have to be in constant communication with the central repository, so working remotely or without an Internet connection is not possible.

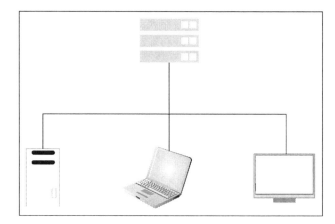

Git

Git is a much younger VCS and has been rising in popularity for a few years now, mostly due to the wide adoption by the open-source community and popularity of Github (www.github.com).

A critical difference between SVN and Git is that Git is a decentralized version control system, which means there is no central authority or main repository; each developer has a full copy of the repository locally available.

Being decentralized makes Git faster in addition to having a better and more powerful branching system than other VCSs; also, working remotely or without an Internet connection is possible.

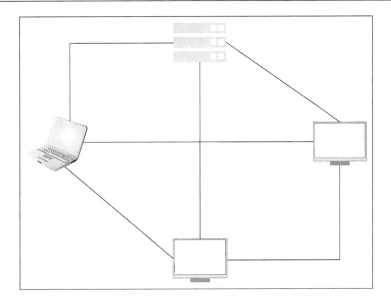

Regardless of which VCS we choose, the most powerful (and sometimes overlooked) feature of any VCS is branching or the ability to create branches.

Branching allows us to experiment and work on new features without breaking the stable code in our trunk or master; creating a branch requires us to take a snapshot of the current trunk/master code where we can make any changes and tests.

Now, branching is only part of the equation; once we are comfortable with our code changes and have properly tested every edge case, we need a way of reintegrating those changes into our main code base. Merging gives us this capability to reintegrate all our branch modifications by running a few commands.

By integrating branches and merging changes into our workflow, we gain flexibility and the freedom to work on different set of changes, features, and bug fixes without interfering with experimental or work-in-progress code.

Also, as we will learn next, version control can help us to do seamless promotions and keep our code up to date across multiple Magento installations with ease.

Distribution

You might want to freely distribute your extension or make it available commercially, but how could you guarantee that the code is properly installed each time without having to do it yourself? And what about the updates or upgrades? Not all store owners are tech savvy or capable of changing files on their own.

Fortunately, Magento comes out of the box with its own package manager and extension marketplace called Magento Connect.

Magento Connect allows developers and solution partners to share their open-source and commercial contributions with the community and is not restricted to only custom modules; we can find the following types of resources in the Magento Connect marketplace:

- Modules
- Language packs
- Custom themes

Packing our extension

One of the core features of Magento Connect is allowing us to package our extensions directly from the Magento backend.

To package our extension perform the following steps:

1. Log in to the Magento backend.
2. From the backend, select **System** | **Magento Connect** | **Package Extensions**.

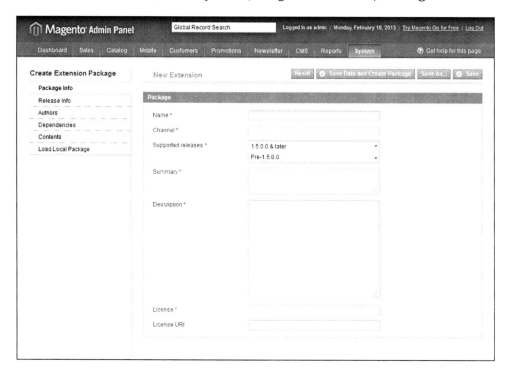

As we can see, the **Create Extension Package** section is composed of six different subsections, which we will cover next.

Package Info

Package Info is used to specify the general extension information such as name, description, and versions of Magento that are supported, as follows:

- **Name**: The standard practice is to keep the name simple and using just words

- **Channel**: This refers to the code pool for the extension; as we mentioned in the previous chapters, extensions designed for distribution should use the "community" channel

- **Supported releases**: Select which version of Magento should be supported for our extension

- **Summary**: This field contains a brief description of the extension used on the extension review process

- **Description**: This has a detailed description of the extension and its functionality

- **License**: This has the license used for this extension; some of the available options are:

  ◦ **Open Software License (OSL)**

  ◦ **Mozilla Public License (MPL)**

  ◦ **Massachusetts Institute of Technology License (MITL)**

  ◦ **GNU General Public License (GPL)**

  ◦ Any other license if your extension is to be distributed commercially

- **License URI**: This has the link to the license text

 More information about the different license types can be found at http://www.magedevguide.com/license-types.

Release Info

The following screenshot shows the screen for **Release Info**:

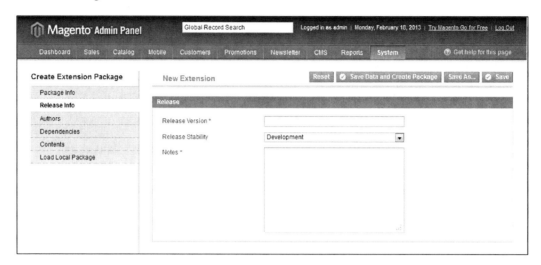

The **Release Info** section contains important data about the current package release:

- **Release Version**: The initial release can be any arbitrary number, however, it is important that the version is incremented with each release. Magento Connect will not allow you to update the same version twice.

- **Release Stability**: Three options are available – **Stable**, **Beta**, and **Alpha**.

- **Notes**: Here we can enter all the release-specific notes, if any.

Authors

The following screenshot shows the screen for **Authors**:

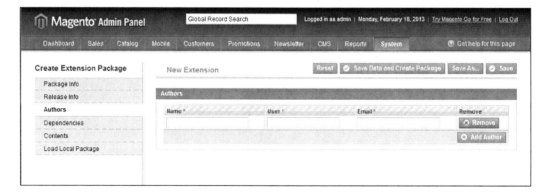

In this section, the information about author(s) is specified; each author's information has the following fields:

- **Name**: Author's full name
- **User**: Magento username
- **Email**: Contact e-mail address

Dependencies

The following screenshot shows the screen for **Dependencies**:

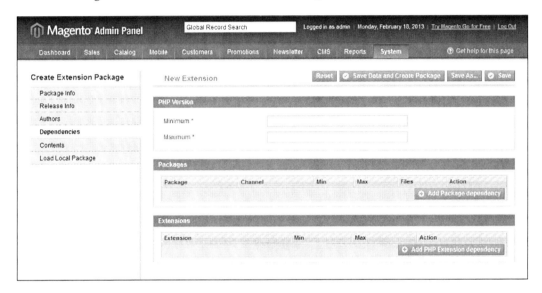

There are three types of dependencies that are used when packaging a Magento extension:

- **PHP Version**: Here we need to specify minimum and maximum versions of PHP that are supported for this extension in the **Minimum** and **Maximum** fields, respectively
- **Packages**: This is used to specify any other packages that are required for this extension
- **Extensions**: Here we can specify if a specific PHP extension is required for our extension to work

In case a package dependency is not met, Magento Connect will allow us to install the required extension; for PHP extensions Magento Connect will throw an error and will stop the installation.

Contents

The following screenshot shows the screen for **Contents**:

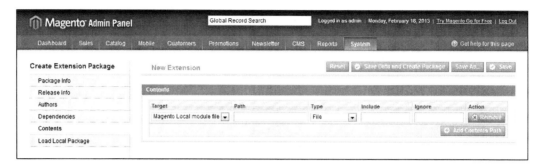

The **Contents** section allows us to specify each file and folder that forms part of the extension package.

 This is the most important section in the extension packaging process and it's also the easiest to mess up.

Each content entry has the following fields:

- **Target**: This is the target base directory and it is used to specify the base path for searching the file. The following options are available:
    - Magento Core team module file – ./app/code/core
    - Magento Local module file – ./app/code/local
    - Magento Community module file – ./app/code/community
    - Magento Global Configuration – ./app/etc
    - Magento Locale language file – ./app/locale
    - Magento User Interface (layouts, templates) – ./app/design
    - Magento Library file – ./lib
    - Magento Media library – ./media
    - Magento Theme Skin (Images, CSS, JS) – ./skin
    - Magento Other web accessible file – ./
    - Magento PHPUnit test – ./tests
    - Magento other – ./

- **Path**: This is the filename and/or path relative to our specified target
- **Type**: For this field, two options are available to us – **File** or **Recursive dir**

- **Include**: This field takes a regular expression that allows us to specify which files to include

- **Ignore**: This field takes a regular expression that allows us to specify which files to exclude

Load Local Package

The following screenshot shows the screen for **Load Local Package**:

This section will allow us to load packaged extensions; since we have not packaged any extensions, the list is currently empty.

Let's go ahead and package our gift registry extension. Be sure to fill in all the fields and then click on **Save Data and Create Package**; this will package and save the extension in the `magento_root/var/connect/` folder.

The extension package file contains all the source's files and the source code needed; additionally, a new file called `package.xml` is created with each package. This file contains all the information about the extension and the detailed structure of the files and folders.

Publishing our extension

Finally, in order to make our extension available, we have to create an extension profile in Magento Connect. To create an extension profile, perform the following steps:

1. Log in to `magentocommerce.com`.

2. Click on the **My Account** link.

3. Click on the **Developers** link in the left-hand side navigation.

4. Click on **Add new extension**.

The **Add new extension** window looks something like the following screenshot:

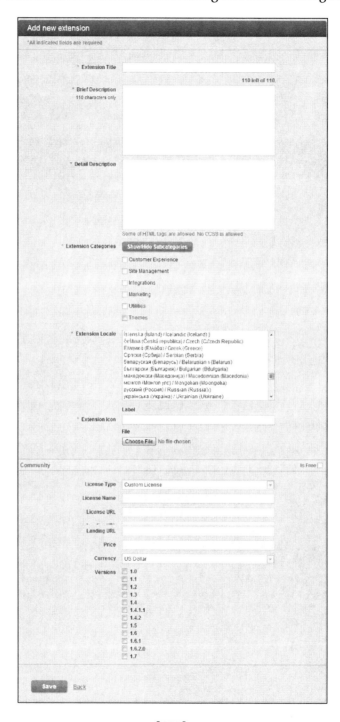

It is important to note that the **Extension Title** field must be the exact name you used while generating the package.

Once the extension profile has been created, we can proceed to upload our extension package; all the fields should match the ones specified during the extension packaging process.

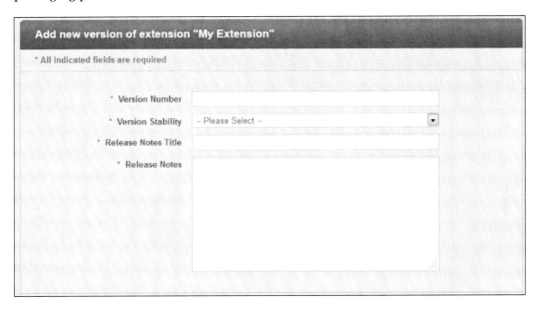

Finally, once we are done, we can click on the **Submit for Approval** button. An extension can have the following status:

- **Submitted**: This means the extension was submitted for review
- **Not Approved**: This means there was a problem with the extension, and you will also receive an e-mail explaining the reason why the extension was not approved
- **Live**: This means the extension has been approved and is available through Magento Connect
- **Offline**: This means you can take your extension offline at any time from your account **Extension Manager**

Summary

In this chapter, we learned how to deploy and share our custom extensions. There are many different methods that we can use for sharing and deploying our code to production environments.

This is the final chapter of our book; we have learned a lot about Magento development, and though we have covered a lot of ground, this book is only meant to be just a stepping stone of your long journey.

Magento is not an easy framework to learn, and while it can be a daunting experience, I encourage you to keep trying and learning.

Hello Magento

The following example will give you a quick and easy introduction into the world of creating Magento extensions. We will create a simple Hello World module that will allow us to display a Hello World! message when we visit a specific URL in our store.

The configuration

Creating a bare bones extension in Magento requires at least two files: `config.xml` and the module declaration file. Let's go ahead and create each one of our files.

The first file is used to declare the module to Magento; without this file, Magento will not be aware of any extension files.

The file location is `app/etc/modules/Mdg_Hello.xml`. Refer to the following code:

```xml
<?xml version="1.0"?>
<config>
    <modules>
        <Mdg_Hello>
            <active>true</active>
            <codePool>local</codePool>
        </Mdg_Hello>
    </modules>
</config>
```

The second XML file is called `config.xml`; it is used to specify all the extension configurations, such as routes, blocks, models, and helper class names. For our example, we are only going to be working with the controllers and the routes.

Let's create the configuration file with the following code.

The file location is `app/code/local/Mdg/Hello/etc/config.xml`. Refer to the following code:

```xml
<?xml version="1.0"?>
<config>
    <modules>
        <Mdg_Hello>
            <version>0.1.0</version>
        </Mdg_Hello>
    </modules>
    <frontend>
        <routers>
            <mdg_hello>
                <use>standard</use>
                <args>
                    <module>Mdg_Hello</module>
                    <frontName>hello</frontName>
                </args>
            </mdg_hello>
        </routers>
    </frontend>
</config>
```

Our extension can now be loaded by Magento, and you can enable or disable our extension in the Magento Backend at **System | Configuration | Advanced**.

The controller

Magento at its core is a **Model-View-Controller (MVC)** framework. So, in order to make our new route functional, we have to create a new controller that will respond to this specific route. To do so, follow these steps:

1. Navigate to the extension root directory.
2. Create a new folder called `controllers`.
3. Inside the `controllers` folder, create a file called `IndexController.php`.
4. Copy the following code (the file location is `app/code/local/Mdg/Hello/controllers/IndexController.php`):

   ```php
   <?php
   class Mdg_Hello_IndexController extends Mage_Core_Controller_Front_Action
   {
   ```

```
    public function indexAction()
{
    echo 'Hello World this is the default action';
    }
}
```

Testing the route

Now that we have created our router and controller, we can test it out by opening `http://magento.localhost.com/hello/index/index`, for which we should see the following screenshot:

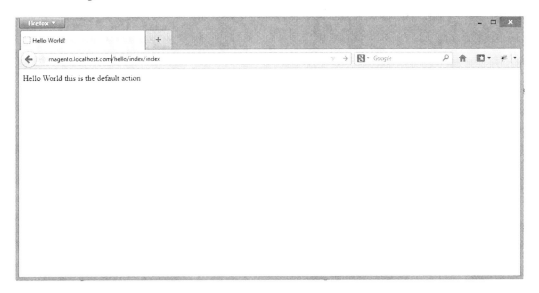

By default, Magento will use both the index controller and the index action as defaults for each extension. So, if we go to `http://magento.localhost.com/hello/`, we should see the same screen.

To conclude our introduction to Magento Module, let's add a new route to our controller:

1. Navigate to the extension root directory.
2. Open `IndexController.php`.

3. Copy the following code (the file location is `app/code/local/Mdg/Hello/controllers/IndexController.php`):

```php
<?php
class Mdg_Hello_IndexController extends Mage_Core_Controller_
Front_Action
{
    public function indexAction()
  {
    echo 'Hello World this is the default action';
    }

    public function developerAction()
    {
        echo 'Hello Developer this is a custom controller
action';
    }
}
```

Finally, let's test it out and load the new action route by going to `http://magento.localhost.com/hello/index/developer` as shown in the following screenshot:

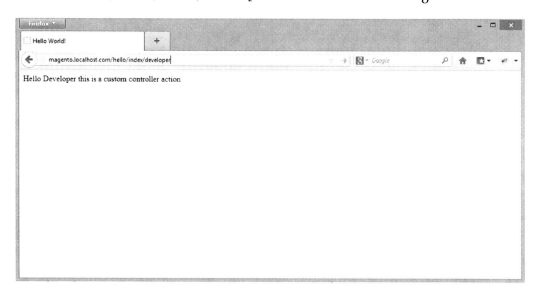

Index

packages, dependencies 221
path field, contents 222
PHP
  about 16
  installing 16
PHP Hypertext Processor 16
PhpStorm 24
PHP Version, dependencies 221
port type, WSDL 163
port, WSDL 163
preDispatch() function 110
product
  deleting 174
  deleting, in SOAPv2 174
  deleting, in XML-RPC 174
products
  adding, to registry 132

R

registries
  managing 145, 146
registry entity table 91
registry item 91
registry item table 91
registry model 91
registry type table 91
regression testing 192
Release Info
  license 220
  notes 220
  release stability 220
  release version 220
release stability, release info 220
release version, release info 220
remote procedure call (RPC) protocol 162
request flow 34
request handling 33-38
Resource Model class 59
REST
  product data, retrieving from staging
    store 172
REST API
  extending 185, 187
RESTful API
  about 166
  credentials, setting up 169, 170

defining 166
features 166
RESTful web service 166
resultsAction() 115
Return Merchandise Authorization (RMA)
    system 66
roles control 167
route
  adding, to controller 229, 230
  setting up 107
  testing 229
routers 33

S

SahiDriver 208
Save Role button 168
search controller
  blocks and views, adding 127-130
  creating 115, 116
Selenium2Driver 208
SeleniumDriver 208
service, WSDL 163
setup resources
  about 97
  creating 97
  defining 98, 99
  Installer Script, creating 99-106
Simple Object Access Protocol (SOAP)
  about 163
  Core API credentials, setting up for 167-169
  URL 163
SOAPv2
  filters, adding to product list call 172
  product, deleting 174
Submit for Approval button 225
Subversion. See SVN
summary, Package info 219
supported releases, Package info 219
SVN 216
Symfony 38

T

target field, contents 222
TDD
  about 193
  with Magento, URL 193

Thank you for buying
Magento PHP Developer's Guide

About Packt Publishing

Packt, pronounced 'packed', published its first book "*Mastering phpMyAdmin for Effective MySQL Management*" in April 2004 and subsequently continued to specialize in publishing highly focused books on specific technologies and solutions.

Our books and publications share the experiences of your fellow IT professionals in adapting and customizing today's systems, applications, and frameworks. Our solution based books give you the knowledge and power to customize the software and technologies you're using to get the job done. Packt books are more specific and less general than the IT books you have seen in the past. Our unique business model allows us to bring you more focused information, giving you more of what you need to know, and less of what you don't.

Packt is a modern, yet unique publishing company, which focuses on producing quality, cutting-edge books for communities of developers, administrators, and newbies alike. For more information, please visit our website: www.packtpub.com.

About Packt Open Source

In 2010, Packt launched two new brands, Packt Open Source and Packt Enterprise, in order to continue its focus on specialization. This book is part of the Packt Open Source brand, home to books published on software built around Open Source licences, and offering information to anybody from advanced developers to budding web designers. The Open Source brand also runs Packt's Open Source Royalty Scheme, by which Packt gives a royalty to each Open Source project about whose software a book is sold.

Writing for Packt

We welcome all inquiries from people who are interested in authoring. Book proposals should be sent to author@packtpub.com. If your book idea is still at an early stage and you would like to discuss it first before writing a formal book proposal, contact us; one of our commissioning editors will get in touch with you.

We're not just looking for published authors; if you have strong technical skills but no writing experience, our experienced editors can help you develop a writing career, or simply get some additional reward for your expertise.

Magento: Beginner's Guide

ISBN: 978-1-84719-594-4   Paperback: 300 pages

Create a dynamic, fully featured, online store with the most powerful open source e-commerce software

1. Step-by-step guide to building your own online store

2. Focuses on the key features of Magento that you must know to get your store up and running

3. Customize the store's appearance to make it uniquely yours

4. Clearly illustrated with screenshots and a working example

Mastering Magento

ISBN: 978-1-84951-694-5   Paperback: 300 pages

Maximize the power of Magento: for developers, designers, and store owners

1. Learn how to customize your Magento store for maximum performance

2. Exploit little known techniques for extending and tuning your Magento installation

3. Step-by-step guides for making your store run faster, better and more productively

Please check **www.PacktPub.com** for information on our titles

Magento Mobile How-to [Instant]

ISBN: 978-1-84969-366-0   Paperback: 78 pages

Create and configure your own Magento Mobile application and publish it for the Andriod and iOS platform

1. Learn something new in an Instant! A short, fast, focused guide delivering immediate results.

2. Style and theme your Magento Mobile Application interface

3. Configure Product categories and add static content for mobile

4. Prepare and publish your Magento mobile application targeting iPhone/iPad and Android platforms

Magento 1.3 Sales Tactics Cookbook

ISBN: 978-1-84951-012-7   Paperback: 292 pages

Improve your Magento store's sales and increase your profits with this collection of simple and effective tactical techniques

1. Build a professional Magento sales web site, with the help of easy-to-follow steps and ample screenshots, to solve real-world business needs and requirements

2. Develop your web site by using your creativity and exploiting the sales techniques that suit your needs

3. Provide visitors with attractive and innovative features to make your site sell

Please check **www.PacktPub.com** for information on our titles

CPSIA information can be obtained at www.ICGtesting.com
Printed in the USA
BVOW060739100613

322883BV00003B/19/P